A Shower of Divine Compassion

A Shower of Divine Compassion

The Collected Poems

of His Divine Grace
A. C. Bhaktivedanta Swami Prabhupāda
Founder-Ācārya of the
International Society for Kṛṣṇa Consciousness

Compiled and translated
by Daśaratha-suta Dāsa

BHAKTIVEDANTA BOOK TRUST

Readers interested in the subject matter of this book are invited by the Bhaktivedanta Book Trust to correspond with its secretary at the following address:

Bhaktivedanta Book Trust
Hare Krishna Land,
Juhu, Mumbai 400 049, India.

Website / E-mail :
www.indiabbt.com
admin@indiabbt.com

A Shower of Divine Compassion (English)

1st printing, February 2009 : 3,000 copies
2nd printing, February 2023 : 3,000 copies

ISBN : 978-81-958860-2-9

Published and Printed by the Bhaktivedanta Book Trust.

ET6N

To the devotees of
His Divine Grace

Contents

FOREWORD

Just when Śrīla Prabhupāda's followers might have thought that all his literary works had been gathered and published, we are surprised and pleased to receive this complete collection of his poetry, compiled and translated by Daśaratha-suta Prabhu. It is not that ISKCON has never seen these poems; Śrīla Prabhupāda himself presented some of them to his disciples, and others have been available in the Bengali *Vaiṣṇava Songbook* for years. Now, however, for the first time they have been collected in one book and presented in English.

Śrīla Prabhupāda usually wrote in English, even before coming to the West in 1965, because his spiritual master ordered him to preach in English. Therefore it is significant that with the exceptions of the homage beginning *Adore, Adore Ye All* in English and the *Praṇāma Śloka for Śrī Keśava Mahārāja* in Sanskrit, the rest of the poems were written in Prabhupāda's native Bengali. From this we can surmise that the poems were outpourings of his heart. It is only fitting that personal emotions be recorded in the poet's own language.

The poems were written in rhyming couplets, the music of which, unfortunately, does not survive in translation. What does survive, however, is the meaning, and despite the difficulties inherent in translating poetry, Daśaratha-suta Prabhu has provided us with clear, precise renderings for our consideration and contemplation.

As personal expression, poetry may provide an intimate exchange between poet and reader. Abhinava Gupta, the influential commentator on *Nāṭya-śāstra*, explains that the scriptures educate us as a master teaches: through unequivocal commands; the histories educate us as a friend teaches: by putting philosophy into the context of case studies; and poetic literature educates us as a lover teaches: by filling us with the joy of expression and the privacy of a moment shared, so that our spiritual aspirations soar and we barely notice the instruction's presence.

Śrīla Prabhupāda has given us authoritative scriptures to command us, and he has also provided many case histories by which we could understand them. His poetry, written in the privacy of his own heart, is a special gift. Not every author attempts to contain his heart in his writings in a poetic form; in poetry one often speaks a subjective truth and of subjective experience. To capture such personal epiphanies requires the spirit of a poet.

Each of the poems reveals both autobiographical data and especially a particular mood or emotion that Śrīla Prabhupāda experienced at that time. After he left his family and business and moved alone to Vṛndāvana with no material support, he laughs at his "list of names." Such human expression from the greatest of devotees! If we open ourselves to that humanness, as he has described it – not in a treatise on surrender but in a personal and soulful expression – we can catch a glimpse of his heart.

Similarly, we can taste his frustration in the poems addressed to or written about his godbrothers, in which he criticizes the dismantling of his *guru's* mission. We can also hear his cry of separation from Śrīla Bhaktisiddhānta Sarasvatī Ṭhākura, as in his refrain: "*O Śrīla Prabhupāda! You personally suffer/ to see the suffering/ of the fallen conditioned souls./ On this day of your separation/ I am utterly despondent.*" We can feel the fervor of his calling out to *guru* and Kṛṣṇa aboard the *Jaladuta*, and be touched by his apparent helplessness when he arrived at the Boston pier and for the first time saw the degradation of Western culture: "*I can guess that You have some work to do here,/ otherwise, why should You bring me/ to such a terrible place?. . . If you have brought me here to dance, O Lord,/ then make me dance, make me dance./ O Lord, make me dance as You like.*"

Such expressions are unique in Prabhupāda's writings, and they reveal the pure devotee's private nature: he is never confident in his own abilities, but always dependent on Kṛṣṇa. Hearing that dependence expressed in prayerful poetry can touch a chord in our heart. Spoken from the poet's immediate experience, such expressions can inspire us – as a lover inspires us – with joy and hope and a renewed determination to surrender ourselves at our Beloved's feet. A poem, like an arrow, should penetrate the heart and make the head spin, and Śrīla Prabhupāda's poems have that power.

In a sense, these poems are footnotes to Śrīla Prabhupāda's voluminous writings, lectures, and conversations, but we are grateful to have them. It could be said that Prabhupāda's books are actually Śrīla Vyāsadeva's revelation, though his purports are certainly expressions, as he said, of his own "personal ecstasies." His poems are particularly his own revelations in a way that his books are not. We hear him speak so personally to his Kṛṣṇa: *"O my dear brother! In Your company/ I will experience great joy once again./ Wandering about the pastures and fields,/ I will pass the entire day with You in tending the cows./ Running and frolicking with You throughout the many forests of Vraja,/ I will enjoy our pastime of stealing and eating one another's lunch./ When, oh when, will that day be mine?"* This is a glimpse not only into what is universally true to all souls, but into the absolute truth of Śrīla Prabhupāda's own experience. As his followers, we are always eager to gain access to these private moments with Prabhupāda. Śrīla Prabhupāda is our spiritual master, and the eternal *guru* has unlimited depths and personal exchanges with his purified disciples. We approach Śrīla Prabhupāda through whatever gates he has provided, and this poetry provides a way to know him in his privacy.

An important point to note is how poetry fares in translation. In the strictest sense, poetry is not translated but rendered into another language. Poetry is by nature filled with the nuances of language, and such nuances defy translation. Thus what we have in this book is a rendering, a capturing of the spirit of the original. Śrīla Prabhupāda similarly said of his translation of *Caitanya-caritāmṛta*, "We are trying to present *Śrī Caitanya-caritāmṛta* in English and do not know how successful it will be, but if one reads the original *Caitanya-caritāmṛta* in Bengali he will relish increasing ecstasy in devotional service." (Cc. Ādi 8.39, purport) As the full music of Prabhupāda's expressions remain inaccessible to those who do not read Bengali, so the full music of the *Caitanya-caritāmṛta* can be most appreciated in its original language. Śrīla Bhaktisiddhānta Sarasvatī Ṭhākura predicted that Westerners would learn Bengali just to hear that music in the *Caitanya-caritāmṛta*. Therefore I suggest that those who read *this* book spend time with the Bengali presented before the translations so that they will have the opportunity to follow the images, metaphors, and vocabulary. What we are given in translation is only a residue of song. Even that residue, however, is enough for us to hear Prabhupāda's music. This is the power of poetry: it spans the superficial barriers of time, language, and culture, and articulates the human soul's truest music.

Now that we have enumerated some difficulties in translating poetry, I wish to add that what qualifies a translator is that he has learned to read well. Every translation requires interpretation. Therefore, if the translator has not thoroughly studied the poet's life and teachings, his interpretation will not be true and transparent. That Daśaratha-suta Prabhu has done his homework is evidenced by his rendering of Śrīla Prabhupāda's poems.

Satsvarūpa Dāsa Goswami

Translator's Note

With great reverence we place before you this anthology of Śrīla Prabhupāda's poems. Most are written in Bengali, one is in English, and the final one is in Sanskrit.

All the Bengali poems are currently included in the ISKCON Māyāpur Bengali songbook, *Bhakti Gīti Sañcayana,* and are well known and sung by the Bengali devotees. However, they have been inaccessible to English-speaking devotees, even though more than thirty years have passed since Śrīla Prabhupāda's disappearance, in 1977. I pray that these confidential writings of our spiritual master, finally coming to light at this late hour, may increase the devotional mood of devotees worldwide.

The title, *A Shower of Divine Compassion,* was suggested by a devotee who read the fourth verse of Śrīla Prabhupāda's Invocation from the *Gītāra Gāna,* wherein he describes that he was sprinkled with the shower of his spiritual master's causeless mercy.

Several of these poems were previously published by the Bhaktivedanta Book Trust in the Vyāsa-pūjā books offered annually on Śrīla Prabhupāda's appearance anniversary. Prabhupāda's English poem, starting *Adore, adore ye all,* has appeared at the beginning of the Vyāsa-pūjā book for 1973 and each book from 1975 through 1988. Here in this volume we have also quoted several letters Prabhupāda wrote to his disciples in which he mentions the poem, and we have included an explanation of the poem that he gave in a lecture in 1976.

The two poems written in 1965 aboard the steamship *Jaladuta* during Prabhupāda's journey to the United States have appeared in the Vyāsa-pūjā books for 1976 and 1979 and were also printed in *Songs of the Vaiṣṇava Ācāryas* in 1979, in accordance with Prabhupāda's request. However, the 1989 edition of *Songs of the Vaiṣṇava Ācāryas,* currently in print, omits these two poems.

We noticed slight differences in some of the wordings of these poems as printed in the ISKCON Bengali songbook, in early editions of *Back to Godhead* magazine, and in Śrīla Prabhupāda's letters. The first of the two poems has no title in Śrīla Prabhupāda's original handwriting. In a letter in 1976 he suggested that it be called *Prayer to the Lotus Feet of Kṛṣṇa*, and a disciple dubbed it *Bhagavān Kṛṣṇera Pāda-Padme Prārthanā*. The second poem was titled in Śrīla Prabhupāda's handwriting: *Mārkine Bhāgavata-Dharma*, which translates as *Preaching Kṛṣṇa Consciousness in America*.

We remembered that in the 1970s there had been an unpublished English rendering of *Vṛndāvane Bhajana* by one of Prabhupāda's disciples; after a long and expensive search for it turned up nothing, we began our own translation. Finally an old copy of that early rendering surfaced. Although in a few places it seemed somewhat vague and inaccurate, to honor the efforts of the previous translator we ended up borrowing some choice phrases from it anyway. Śrīla Prabhupāda composed this extensive poem in 108 couplets in 27 sections, and we have created section headings as an outline of the topics on which he was meditating.

An English rendering of *Vaiśiṣṭyāṣṭaka*, done by one of Prabhupāda's early disciples, appeared in the beginning of the Vyāsa-Pūjā books for 1978 and 1982. An old typewritten English rendering of *Viraha-Aṣṭāṣṭaka* was also located. We have upgraded these early translations and made them more precise and current in expression. Also, for each of these two octets, headings for the eight sections have been created as an outline of the themes.

In this anthology we have provided introductions to each of the poems, drawn from the *Śrīla Prabhupāda-līlāmṛta*, by Satsvarūpa Dāsa Goswami. These descriptions provide a glimpse into Śrīla Prabhupāda's situation at the time of writing each poem.

Although Śrīla Prabhupāda's Bengali poems are regularly published in the BBT's Bengali songbook, numerous typographical differences have crept into the text over the years. With great endeavor on the part of many devotees, we eventually collected the oldest available versions, which were mostly scans from the rare *Gauḍīya Patrikā* magazine. Thus we were able to clear up countless discrepancies and resolve significant alterations of the original meaning.

This book was more than twelve years in the making, but we completed most of these translations during a four-year period while living in a rustic cabin at the beautiful Murari-Sevaka farm community in Tennessee. Living without electricity or running water, we typed on a primitive DOS laptop computer, powered by an extra car battery, and used simple oil lamps to work late into the quiet, peaceful nights. This anthology was pieced together on the strength of Śrīla Prabhupāda's causeless mercy, and now we humbly offer it at the lotus feet of His Divine Grace in the hope that he will be pleased with our imperfect presentation. May the devotees relish this book and keep these merciful instructions of Śrīla Prabhupāda always in their hearts!

Daśaratha-suta Dāsa
August 24, 2008
The appearance anniversary
of Śrīla Prabhupāda

Maṅgalācaraṇa
from
Gītāra Gāna

Maṅgalācaraṇa
Auspicious Invocation

from the poem

Śrī Gītāra Gāna
"The Song of the Gītā"

A versified Bengali translation of the
complete *Bhagavad-gītā*, composed in 1962, by
His Divine Grace
A. C. Bhaktivedanta Swami Prabhupāda

Introduction

The other poems in this anthology are in chronological order, but this one is presented out of sequence. We offer it first, as an appropriate invocation, since Śrīla Prabhupāda herein petitions the Supreme Lord and His devotees to guide his writing efforts. This piece was written when he was sixty-six, three years after he accepted the renounced order, *sannyāsa.* Śrīla Prabhupāda had resided in the Vaṁśī-Gopālajī temple in Vṛndāvana since September 1958. Although periodically he traveled to Delhi, Kanpur, Bombay, and other places to preach, Prabhupāda kept returning to the Vaṁśī-Gopālajī temple at this time.

In July 1962, he made a final move in India before departing for the United States in 1965 – from the Vaṁśī-Gopālajī temple to the famous temple of Śrī Śrī Rādhā-Dāmodara, established in Seva Kuñja by Śrīla Jīva Gosvāmī. There Prabhupāda settled in for his marathon effort of translating the *Śrīmad-Bhāgavatam* while living very simply and using a manual typewriter.

During the spring, summer, and fall of 1962, he also managed to complete a translation of the 700-verse Sanskrit *Bhagavad-gītā* into rhyming Bengali couplets, which he called *Gītāra Gāna.* This impressive work was published by his godbrother and *sannyāsa guru,* Keśava Mahārāja, in the *Gauḍīya Patrikā* magazine in three issues: Volume XIV, numbers 4, 7, and 8 (June,

September, and October 1962).

Śrīla Prabhupāda also wrote an extensive introduction in Bengali prose to the *Gītāra Gāna*, which framed the entire work for the masses. Therein he discusses the transcendental reason for Śrīpāda Śaṅkarācārya's spreading Māyāvāda philosophy, and he quotes famous Vaiṣṇava authorities such as Śrīpāda Rāmānujācārya and Śrīla Bhaktivinoda Ṭhākura.

Śrīla Prabhupāda ends each of the eighteen chapters of his versified *Bhagavad-gītā* with a benediction for the reader:

> *bhakati-vedānta gāhe śrī gītāra gāna*
> > *yadi śune śuddha bhakta, kṛṣṇa-gata prāṇa*

> Bhaktivedanta thus recites the poem
> > named *Śrī Gītāra Gāna.*
> Whoever listens to it becomes a purified devotee;
> > his heart becomes endeared to Lord Kṛṣṇa.

MAṄGALĀCARAṆA
AUSPICIOUS INVOCATION

from the poem

Śrī Gītāra Gāna
"The Song of the Gītā"

(1) *śrī-guru-vandanā kari', tāṅhāra caraṇa dhari,*
śrī-bhaktisiddhānta prabhupāda
āra yata śikṣā-guru, sabe vañcā-kalpa-taru,
kṛpā kara ghucuka viṣāda

śrī-guru-vandanā – obeisances to the divine spiritual master; *kari'* – offering; *tāṅhāra caraṇa* – his feet; *dhari* – holding; *śrī-bhaktisiddhānta prabhupāda* – Śrīla Bhaktisiddhānta Sarasvatī Prabhupāda; *āra* – furthermore; *yata* – all; *śikṣā-guru* – instructing spiritual masters; *sabe* – all of them; *vañcā-kalpa-taru* – wish-fulfilling trees; *kṛpā kara* – being merciful; *ghucuka* – may it be relieved; *viṣāda* – sadness.

Clutching the lotus feet of my spiritual master,
Śrīla Bhaktisiddhānta Sarasvatī Prabhupāda,
I offer my respectful obeisances unto him,
as well as unto all of my instructing spiritual masters.
Because they are just like wish-fulfilling trees,
I pray that they may bestow their mercy,
thereby bringing my sadness to an end.

(2) *rūpa-sanātana prabhu, gauḍīya-ācārya vibhu,*
āra sei bhaṭṭa-raghunātha
śrī-jīva-gopāla-bhaṭṭa, vṛndāvane ye saṁghaṭṭa,
mile prabhu dāsa-raghunātha

rūpa-sanātana prabhu – Śrī Rūpa Gosvāmī and Sanātana Gosvāmī; *gauḍīya-ācārya* – among the Gauḍīya Vaiṣṇava leaders; *vibhu* – self-effulgent; *āra* – and; *sei* – that; *bhaṭṭa raghunātha* – Raghunātha Bhaṭṭa Gosvāmī; *śrī-jīva-gopāla-bhaṭṭa* – Śrī Jīva Gosvāmī and Gopāla Bhaṭṭa Gosvāmī; *vṛndāvane* – in Vṛndāvana; *ye* – which; *saṁghaṭṭa* – assembly; *mile* – gathering together; *prabhu dāsa-raghunātha* – Raghunātha Dāsa Gosvāmī.

Śrīla Rūpa Gosvāmī and Sanātana Gosvāmī are the self-effulgent leaders
of all the Gauḍīya Vaiṣṇava *ācāryas*.
With Śrī Raghunātha Bhaṭṭa Gosvāmī, Śrī Jīva Gosvāmī,
Śrī Gopāla Bhaṭṭa Gosvāmī, and Śrī Raghunātha Dāsa Gosvāmī,
they gathered together and associated in Śrī Vṛndāvana-dhāma.

(3) *gosvāmī prabhura gaṇa, āśraya sei śrī-caraṇa,*
anya mora kichu āśā nāi
tāṅra madhye ye śrī-jīva, ujjvala ācārya-dīpa,
diyāchena caraṇete ṭhāi

gosvāmī prabhura – of the Gosvāmī *prabhus*; *gaṇa* – the assembly; *āśraya* – refuge; *sei* –
those; *śrī-caraṇa* – divine feet; *anya* – other; *mora* – my; *kichu* – anything; *āśā* – wish;
nāi – there is not; *tāṅra madhye* – among them all; *ye* – who; *śrī-jīva* – Jīva Gosvāmī;
ujjvala – brilliant; *ācārya-dīpa* – torchlamp for all spiritual masters; *diyāchena* – he has
given; *caraṇete* – by his own feet; *ṭhāi* – a place.

I have no yearning other than for the exclusive shelter
of the lotus feet of these six Gosvāmīs.
Śrīla Jīva Gosvāmī, who is a brilliant torchlamp of knowledge
among all the *ācāryas*,
has mercifully given me a residence
close to his own lotus feet
[in the Rādhā-Dāmodara temple he established].

(4) *āmi se durmati ati, viṣaya-bhogete mati,*
kṛpā kari' ānila ṭāniyā
mūrkha mui nīca ati, śrī-siddhānta sarasvatī,
kṛpā-vāri dila se siñciyā

āmi – I; *se* – such; *durmati* – wicked-minded; *ati* – very much; *viṣaya-bhogete* – in the
enjoyment of sense gratification; *mati* – the mentality; *kṛpā kari'* – showing his mercy;
ānila – has brought; *ṭāniyā* – dragging forcibly; *mūrkha* – a fool; *mui* – me; *nīca ati* – very
low; *śrī-siddhānta sarasvatī* – Śrīla Bhaktisiddhānta Sarasvatī; *kṛpā-vāri* – the shower of
mercy; *dila* – gave; *se* – that; *siñciyā* – sprinkling.

I am a very sinful person, always absorbed
    in the affairs of material sense gratification.
Śrīla Bhaktisiddhānta Sarasvatī has shown great mercy
    by forcibly pulling me out of this unfortunate situation.
I am simply a fool, being very lowly and degraded,
    yet my Guru Mahārāja has kindly sprinkled me
with the shower of his divine compassion.

(5) *patita-pāvana prabhu, nityānanda-gaura vibhu,*
    śrī-advaita kṛpā-pārāvāra
    śrīvāsādi-gadādhara, kṛpā kara e kiṅkara,
    bujhilāma tava kṛpā sāra

patita-pāvana – deliverers of the fallen; *prabhu* – the Lords; *nityānanda-gaura* – Nityānanda and Gaura; *vibhu* – omniscient; *śrī-advaita* – Advaita Prabhu; *kṛpā-pārāvāra* – ocean of mercy; *śrīvāsa-ādi* – devotees headed by Śrīvāsa; *gadādhara* – Gadādhara; *kṛpā kara* – show mercy; *e kiṅkara* – to this servant; *bujhilāma* – I have understood; *tava kṛpā* – Your mercy; *sāra* – essence of life.

O Supreme Lords, deliverers of the fallen!
    O omniscient Lords, Nityānanda-Gaura!
O Śrī Advaita Prabhu, ocean of mercy!
    O Gadadhara! O devotees headed by Śrīvāsa!
Please show mercy to this servant, for I have realized
    that Your mercy is life's essence.

(6) *vṛndāvana ramya-sthāna, sevā-kuñja tāra nāma,*
    śrī-rādhā-dāmodara sthiti
    tāṅhāra caraṇe mui, ekānta āśraya lai,
    kṛpā kari' kara mora gati

vṛndā-vana – the forest of Vṛndā Devī; *ramya-sthāna* – a lovely place; *sevā-kuñja* – the grove Sevā-Kuñja; *tāra nāma* – its name; *śrī-rādhā-dāmodara* – Śrī Rādhā-Dāmodara; *sthiti* – situated; *tāṅhara caraṇe* – at Their feet; *mui* – I; *ekānta āśraya* – exclusive shelter; *lai* – I take; *kṛpā kari'* – showing mercy; *kara* – please be; *mora gati* – my refuge.

Vṛndāvana is a charmingly beautiful place,

   and situated here, in a grove known as Sevā-kuñja,

is the sacred temple of Śrī Śrī Rādhā-Dāmodara.

   I take the lotus feet of these Deities as my only shelter,

and I petition Them to mercifully keep me under Their protection.

(7) *"śrī gītāra gāna" ei, tomāra caraṇe thui,*

   laha mora ei puṣpāñjali

ki jāni ki likhi āmi, ekānta bharasā tumi,

   ye likhāo sei padyāvali

śrī gītāra gāna – the book of poetry named *Śrī Gītāra Gāna*; *ei* – this; *tomāra caraṇe* – at Your feet; *thui* – keeping; *laha* – please accept; *mora* – my; *ei* – this; *puṣpa-añjali* – palmful of flowers; *ki jāni* – whatever I know; *ki likhi* – whatever I write; *āmi* – I; *ekānta* – exclusive; *bharasā* – hope; *tumi* – You; *ye likhāo* – that which You make me write; *sei* – that; *padya-āvali* – series of poetic verses.

O Rādhā-Dāmodara! Please accept this book, **Śrī Gītāra Gāna**,

   as an offering of flowers unto Your lotus feet.

Whatever I know, and whatever I write,

   I am depending exclusively on Your Lordships

and therefore hope it is You dictating these verses.

(8) *abhaya caraṇa tava, āśraye sarvadā ra'ba,*

   ei mora nitya-kāla āśa

"bhakti-vedānta" bale, āmi kintu dāsa ha'le,

   vimocana e māyāra phāṅsa

abhaya – fearless; *caraṇa* – feet; *tava* – Your; *āśraye* – in the shelter; *sarvadā* – always; *ra'ba* – will remain; *ei* – this; *mora* – my; *nitya-kāla* – forever; *āśa* – wish; *bhakti-vedānta* – the poet named Bhaktivedanta; *bale* – says; *āmi* – I; *kintu* – only; *dāsa* – the humble servant; *ha'le* – being; *vimocana* – release; *e* – this; *māyāra phāṅsa* – noose of illusion.

My perpetual desire is to be always situated
    in the shelter of Your lotus feet,
which bestow true fearlessness [*abhaya caraṇa*].
    This poet Bhaktivedanta [also named Abhay Carana] says:
Since I am Your insignificant servant,
    please release me from this illusory noose of *māyā*.

Śrī Vyāsa Pūjā Homage

Śrī Vyāsa Pūjā Homage

**Eight Stanzas on
His Divine Grace 108 Śrī Śrīmad
Bhaktisiddhānta Sarasvatī Gosvāmī Prabhupāda
written in 1935 by
His Divine Grace A. C. Bhaktivedanta Swami Prabhupāda**

Introduction

During 1934 and 1935, Śrīla Prabhupāda (then thirty-eight years old and known as Abhay Charan De) decided that his family should remain in Allahabad while he and his brother went to Bombay, rented an apartment, and evaluated the prospects of starting a pharmaceutical factory. This trip promised to be an extended one, for Abhay and his wife, Rādhārāṇī, had three children, and he would try to build up a large business in Bombay to provide for his growing family. He had first set up a very small manufacturing operation in Allahabad and put his nephew Tulasi in charge, and then left for Bombay with his brother.

In Bombay, Abhay rented an apartment on Grant Road and started his own pharmaceutical factory. In his business travels around Bombay, Abhay met some members of the Gauḍīya Maṭha, and both he and the *sannyāsīs* regarded their meeting as auspicious. These preachers had no permanent center, but they were trying to start one. On behalf of their spiritual master, Śrī Bhaktisiddhānta Sarasvatī, they were going door-to-door soliciting supporters for a Bombay branch of the Gauḍīya Maṭha. Abhay wanted to help. As a fellow godbrother in the service of his spiritual master, he offered them his support. Abhay introduced the *sannyāsīs* to business acquaintances, who gave donations for the new center. Abhay then regularly visited the Maṭha quarters on Proctor Road, where he joined the devotees in *kīrtana* and discussed topics from the *Śrīmad-Bhāgavatam* with them.

February 25, 1935 was the sixty-second birthday of Śrīla Bhaktisiddhānta Sarasvatī. At Jagannātha Purī, where Śrīla Bhaktisiddhānta Sarasvatī was residing, the devotees observed the day with festive celebrations. At the small Bombay center, the few disciples planned an evening observance and invited local people. For the occasion, Abhay wrote an English poem glorifying his spiritual master, beginning with the lines *Adore, adore ye all, the happy day.*

Abhay also composed a long and scholarly speech in English, which he read before the assembled guests and members of the temple. Although his first language was Bengali, his English was clear and natural. Like the poem, the speech was personal, but even more than the poem it was authoritative, philosophical preaching. The godbrothers were impressed to hear Abhay presenting the Vaiṣṇava philosophy so expertly. But he had heard the Vaiṣṇava philosophy from Śrīla Bhaktisiddhānta Sarasvatī, just as they had. And Bhaktisiddhānta favored preaching in English. So why should Abhay not be able to enunciate the teachings of his spiritual master, having heard from him and having read the *Gītā*, *Bhāgavatam*, and *Bhakti-rasāmṛta-sindhu?* But, until now, no one in Bombay knew he could expertly preach in English.

Abhay submitted both the poem and the speech to *The Harmonist*, the devotional journal Bhaktisiddhānta Sarasvatī had established for preaching in the English language. The poem, Abhay's first published work, introduced him as a competent writer in English, and Swami Bhakti-pradīpa Tīrtha, editor of *The Harmonist*, informally dubbed Abhay a *kavi*, or poet. Most of Abhay's godbrothers, even the *sannyāsīs*, were not so proficient in English. They could appreciate that the poem was personal, written out of Abhay's genuine worship of and his joy at having accepted a spiritual master, but it was also written strictly in accord with the conclusions of scriptures.

For Abhay, however, the real glory of his *Śrī Vyāsa Pūjā Homage* came when the poem reached Śrīla Bhaktisiddhānta Sarasvatī, who was greatly pleased with this offering. One stanza specifically made Śrīla Bhaktisiddhānta so happy that he made a point of showing it to many of his guests:

> Absolute is sentient
> Thou hast proved,
> Impersonal calamity
> Thou hast moved.

Somehow in this simple couplet Abhay had captured the essence of his spiritual master's preaching against the Māyāvādīs, and Śrīla Bhaktisiddhānta took it as an indication of how well Abhay knew his mind. Abhay was delighted when he heard that the couplet was pleasing to his spiritual master. One of Abhay's godbrothers compared this verse by Abhay to a verse in which Śrīla Rūpa Gosvāmī had expressed the inner thinking of Lord Caitanya Mahāprabhu and had thus moved Him to ecstasy. Śrīla Bhaktisiddhānta Sarasvatī also found the essay pleasing, and he showed it to some of his confidential devotees. He instructed the editor of *The Harmonist*, "Whatever he writes, publish it."

The following version of the poem was prepared by the BBT from two sources: Śrīla Prabhupāda's March 1952 *Back to Godhead* magazine, and a version he wrote by hand on the back of a letter he sent Rāyarāma Dāsa on March 20, 1969.

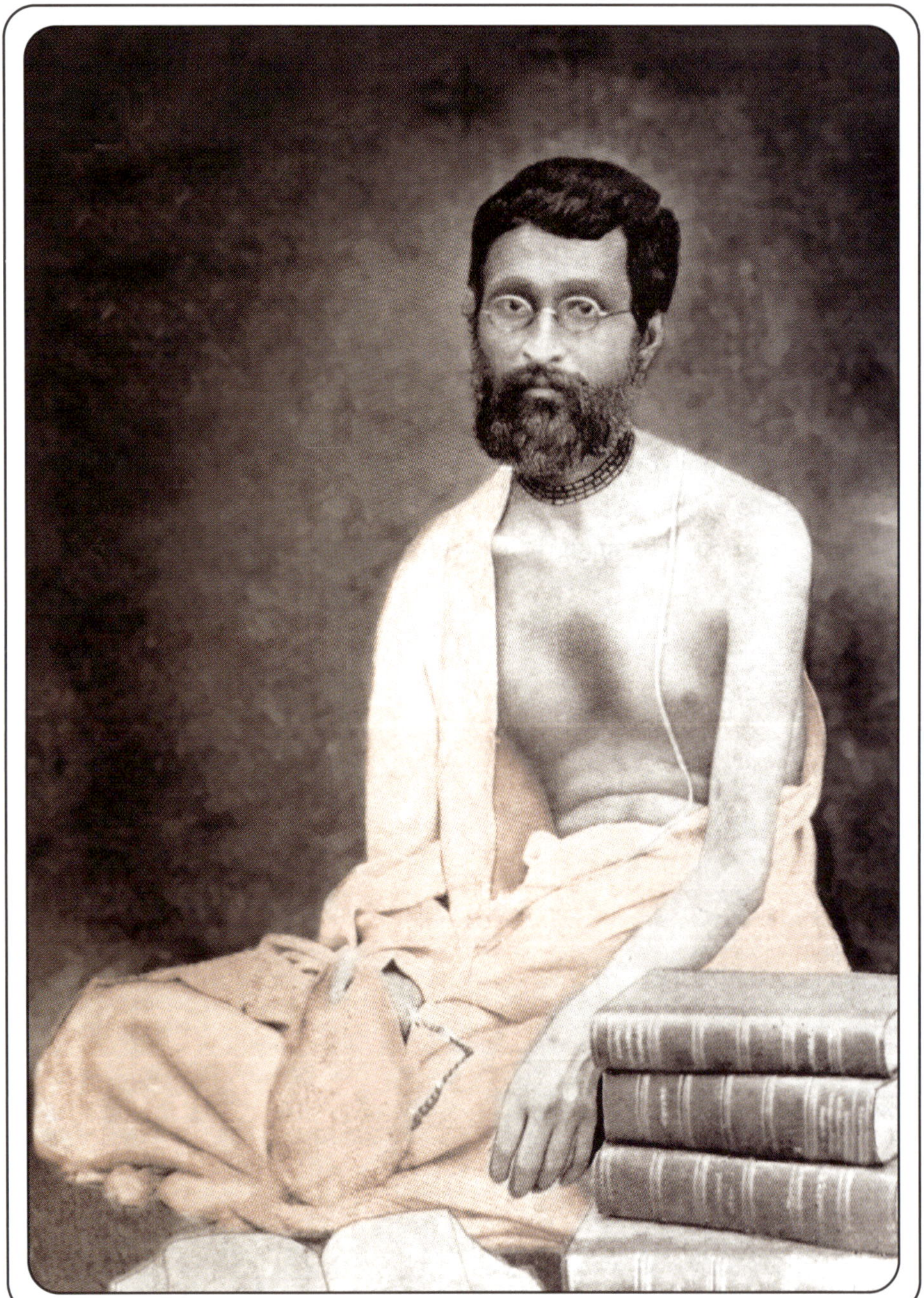

Eight Stanzas on
His Divine Grace 108 Śrī Śrīmad
Bhaktisiddhānta Sarasvatī Gosvāmī Prabhupāda

~ 1 ~

Adore, adore ye all
    The happy day.
Blessed than heaven,
    Sweeter than May,
When He appeared at Puri,
    The holy place,
My lord and master,
    His Divine Grace.

~ 2 ~

Oh my Master,
    The evangelic angel,
Give us thy light,
    Light up thy candle.
Struggle for existence
    A human race.
The only hope,
    Your Divine Grace.

~ 3 ~

Misled we are,
    All going astray.
Save us, lord,
    Our fervent pray.
Wonder thy ways
    To turn our face.
Adore thy feet,
    Your Divine Grace.

~ 4 ~

Forgotten Krishna,
    We fallen souls
Paying most heavy
    The illusion's toll.
Darkness around,
    All distress.
The only hope,
    Your Divine Grace.

~ 5 ~

Message of service
    Thou hast brought,
A meaningful life
    As Chaitanya wrought.
Unknown to all,
    It's full of brace.
That's your gift,
    Your Divine Grace.

~ 6 ~

Absolute is sentient
    Thou hast proved.
Impersonal calamity
    Thou hast removed
This gives a life
    Anew and fresh.
Worship thy feet,
    Your Divine Grace.

~ 7 ~

Had you not come,
    Who had told
The message of Krishna,
    Forceful and bold.
That's your right,
    You have the mace.
Save me, a fallen,
    Your Divine Grace.

~ 8 ~

The line of service
    As drawn by you
Is pleasing and healthy
    Like morning dew.
The oldest of all,
    but in new dress.
Miracle done,
    Your Divine Grace.

—Abhay Charan Dasadhikari

The Lost Poem

The Vyāsa Pūjā poem was published in *The Harmonist* in 1935, and Abhay Charanaravinda Bhaktivedanta later reprinted it in his own magazine, *Back To Godhead*, Part I, Volume IX, dated March 1952. The title of the piece now read:

Paramhansa Sree Sreemad Bhakti Siddhanta
Saraswati Goswami Maharaj

Afterward, he seemed to lose track of the poem among the many papers produced while writing and translating work at the Rādhā-Dāmodara temple. He took *sannyāsa* in 1959, becoming Bhaktivedanta Swami Mahārāja, and set forth for the United States in 1965.

The following is an excerpt from Śrīla Prabhupāda's letter to his American disciple Rāyarāma Dāsa, dated December 14, 1967, in which he mentions the poem:

We may all go together to London and start a branch there in grand scale, so also in Amsterdam and in Berlin or Moscow. We have to save the world-people from the misconception of voidism and impersonalism.

The absolute is sentient Thou hast proved,
all impersonal calamity Thou hast moved.

These lines were presented by me to my spiritual master and he was highly pleased with me. Let me follow the same principle and my Guru Mahārāja will bless me. I have always my good wishes and blessings for you all because you are cooperating in a great mission. Thank you.

Indeed, in 1969, Śrīla Prabhupāda sent a group of American disciples to London to open the first Kṛṣṇa conscious temple there. On that trip,

Gurudāsa somehow located the lost poem in one copy of *The Harmonist*, a stack of which he found at the India House Library in London. Prabhupāda was elated when he received a copy of it in the mail, and he copied it by hand onto the back of his next letter to Rāyarāma Dāsa, who served on the staff of *Back To Godhead* magazine. That letter was dated March 20, 1969, and Śrīla Prabhupāda drew attention to the poem on the back by writing at the bottom of the typed letter:

> On the other side you will find a poetry composed by me in 1935 on the occasion of my Spiritual Master's birthday. This poetry was found in the India House Library at London by Gurudāsa. I was searching after it and my master has rewarded me of this after so long a time (34 years). Please publish it in BTG.

While writing the poem on the back of the letter, Prabhupāda slightly changed some of the words and punctuation. For example, the famous line "Impersonal calamity Thou hast moved" was changed to "Impersonal calamity Thou hast removed." And for the title of the piece he wrote:

Eight Stanzas on His Divine Grace 108 Śrī Śrīmad
Bhaktisiddhānta Sarasvatī Gosvāmī Prabhupāda (1935)

Rāyarāma included the poem in *Back To Godhead #27* in 1969. Much later, on the disappearance anniversary of Bhaktisiddhānta Gosvāmī on December 10, 1976, Śrīla Prabhupāda described his 1935 Vyāsa-pūjā poem in the following talk, in Hyderabad, India, and he expounded on several of its verses.

Śrīla Prabhupāda Explains His 1935 Vyāsa-Pūjā Homage on the Disappearance Day of Śrīla Bhaktisiddhānta Sarasvatī (Hyderabad, December 10, 1976)

Prabhupāda [*reading from* Back To Godhead]: ". . . simple expression of reverence and love. The disciple, Abhay Charan Dāsa, was to become His Divine Grace A. C. Bhaktivedanta Swami Prabhupāda, founder-*ācārya* of the International Society, Kṛṣṇa Consciousness." So whatever I appreciated forty years ago, the same principle is going on. We have no change. What I understood my spiritual master – practically I met him in 1922 and this poetry was written in 1936. That means fourteen years before writing this poetry, I met my Guru Mahārāja in 1922. At that time I was quite a young man, twenty-five years old only, and I was posted in a very responsible position as the office manager of Dr. Bose's laboratory. And I was fond of in those days, of Gandhi's movement. In 1922 I joined Gandhi's movement, and I gave up my educational career because one of Gandhi's programs was to boycott the universities. That's a very long story. And many students gave up their educational career and joined this Gandhi's movement, and I was one of them.

So Dr. Bose, Kartik Chandra Bose, he was a very important man. At that time he was the managing director of Bengal Chemical Company. Now there is a street in central Calcutta: Dr. Kartik Bose Street. So he was very important man, and he was our family physician and my father's very intimate friend. So when I gave up my education and I was joining Gandhi's movement, at that time Dr. Kartik Chandra Bose asked me to join him. So with the permission of my father I joined. So I was fond of, at that time, this Gandhi's noncooperation movement. And then, when I joined Dr. Bose's laboratory, of course, I was dressed in *khaddar*. So Dr. Bose liked that dress, *khaddar* dress. He told me one day that "Out of your whole Gandhi's movement, I like this *khaddar* only." Dr. Bose said. And why? "No, because this will give impetus to industry. This hand-spinning will gradually give impetus to India." Actually that happened. He was himself an industrialist. Actually in India the chemical industry was given birth by Dr. Kartik Chandra Bose.

He was very important man. He started this Bengal Chemical.

So, 1922, I met my Guru Mahārāja through the exigency of my intimate friend, Mr. Narendranath Mullick. And I would not go. He told me information, "There is a nice *sādhu*. Let us go and see." I did not like very much these *sādhus* in those days – national spirit. So I said, "I have seen many *sādhus*. They come at my father's care. I was not very much pleased with their behavior." So he dragged me forcibly: "No, I have heard this person is very exalted." So I went. And his first opening version was that "You are educated young men. Why don't you preach Caitanya Mahāprabhu's gospel in the Western countries?" I did not know. So this was his blessing in the first meeting. I did not know, but because we belonged to a Vaiṣṇava family we were very much worshiper of Lord Caitanya and Nityānanda, our family Deity. So I was very much pleased that "Here is a personality who is going to preach Caitanya Mahāprabhu's gospel." I was very much pleased.

So anyway from 1922 to 1933 practically I was not initiated, but I got the impression of preaching Caitanya Mahāprabhu's cult. That I was thinking. And that was the initiation by my Guru Mahārāja. Then officially I was initiated in 1933, because in 1923 I left Calcutta. I started my business at Allahabad. So I was always thinking of my Guru Mahārāja that "I met a very nice *sādhu*." Although I was doing business, I never forgot him. Then, in 1928, these Gauḍīya Maṭha people came to Allahabad during Kumbha Mela. As the Kumbha Mela is going to be held this year, a similar big Kumbha Mela was held in 1928. In those days they came to open their branch in Allahabad, and somebody recommended that "You go to . . ." At that time I was running on my big pharmacy and I was very well-known man in Allahabad as the proprietor of the pharmacy. So somebody recommended them that "You go to Abhay Babu. He is a very religious man. He'll help you." So when they entered my shop I was very much pleased: "These men I met in 1922, and now they have come." In this way I became reconnected.

And in 1933 I was officially initiated, and my only qualification was when I was introduced to my Guru Mahārāja for initiation, so Guru Mahārāja immediately said, "Yes, I shall initiate this boy. He is very nice. He hears me very patiently. He does not go away." So that was my qualification. The high standard of philosophy which he was speaking at that time, practically I could not follow what he was speaking, but still I liked to hear him. That was my hobby. I was asking, "When Guru Mahārāja will speak?" So he took it very seriously. And then, in 1936 – it's a long history – during this Vyāsa-pūjā day, this Vyāsa-pūjā day, whatever I studied about our relationship with my Guru Mahārāja I expressed in this poetry, and since that day my godbrothers used to call me "poet".

And Guru Mahārāja also very much appreciated this poetry. Now somehow or other you have found it [*laughs*]. I thought the poetry is lost, but I do not know how it was found out by some of our disciples. I think it was found out in London museum or somewhere else by Gurudāsa. They had a stock of *Harmonist*, and from the *Harmonist*, my Guru Mahārāja's paper, this poetry was found. Otherwise, I thought it was lost. So anyway this poetry is

> **"Adore, adore ye all, the happy day,**
>
> **Blessed than heaven, sweeter than May."**

So I heard that the month of May is very pleasing in the Western countries, so I compared the happiness of this day with the May Day. They call May Day?

Devotees: Yes.

Prabhupāda: Yes.

> **"When he appeared at Puri, the holy place,**
>
> **My lord and master, His Divine Grace."**

So Bhaktisiddhānta Sarasvatī Ṭhākura appeared as the son of Bhaktivinoda Ṭhākura, his fourth son. Bhaktivinoda Ṭhākura, he was family man. He had several children, sons and daughters. So Bhaktisiddhānta Sarasvatī Ṭhākura, known in his previous life as Bimala Prasāda Datta, son of Kedaranātha Datta. His father, Bhaktivinoda Ṭhākura, his name was. He was magistrate and he was manager also, the managing board of Jagannatha Puri. The system is that the local magistrate becomes the official manager of the managing board of Jagannatha Puri. So at that time he was situated in Jagannatha Puri, and Bhaktisiddhānta Sarasvatī Ṭhākura appeared at Puri. And the Ratha-yātrā, the Ratha-yātrā ceremony takes place, and sometimes the big *ratha* stops at interval. So the house in which Bhaktisiddhānta

Sarasvatī Ṭhākura appeared, in front of that house the *ratha* stopped.

So his mother took the advantage, and because Bhaktivinoda Ṭhākura was magistrate, so the son, the little baby, was brought before the *ratha*, and the *pūjārīs* allowed him to bring the child before the Deity. And the child was placed before the Deity, and a garland was offered by Jagannātha. So that was the first sign of his becoming the *ācārya*. In this way there are many incidences. So therefore his birthplace is mentioned,

> "... the holy place,
> **My lord and master, His Divine Grace.**
> **O my master, the evangelic angel,**
> **Give us thy light, light up thy candle.**
> **Struggle for existence, a human race,**
> **The only hope, His Divine Grace."**

So actually we are in a very precarious condition, the modern civilization, I mean to say, manipulated by the Western people. It is a soul-killing civilization, this civilization. By nature the chance is given after many, many evolutionary process: *jalaja nava lakṣāṇi sthāvara lakṣa viṁśati.*

The evolutionary theory is there in the *Padma Purāṇa.* It is not Darwin's theory. Darwin might have stolen it from *Padma Purāṇa,* and he presented in a distorted way of his own imagination. Otherwise, the Darwin's theory is not the original. It is not theory, it is fact. *Jīva jātiṣu.* The soul is wandering within the cycle of *jīva jāti,* different species of life. *Tathā dehāntara prāptiḥ.* This is Vedic knowledge, this evolutionary process. It is not Darwin's theory. So by that process, lower animals and then the chronological order is there. First of all aquatics, *jalaja. Jalaja* means aquatic. Then *sthāvara,* trees, plants. Then flies, then birds, then beasts, then human being. In this way, *bahu sambhavānte,* after many, many millions of years we get this opportunity of human life to realize God. And this civilization is denying, refusing the opportunity to the human society to understand God. Such a soul-killing civilization! It is a fact. They are denying: "What is God? There is no God. Everything is science," although they cannot explain science. They cannot do anything, simply talking like nonsense. Last night some girls came, so they are students of botany. So I asked them, can you manufacture a seed which can give birth to a big banyan tree? "No, sir, it is not possible." Then what kind of botany you are studying?

Actually what is their science? They talk simply something which is going on in the middle portion. Where is the beginning and where is the end of knowledge, that they do not know. They are theorizing only in the middle. They do not know *janmādy asya yataḥ*, where is the beginning of this science. Beginning is Kṛṣṇa. Kṛṣṇa says, *ahaṁ sarvasya prabhavo*. He is the beginning. *Bījo 'haṁ sarva-bhūtānām*. That seed, you scientist, you cannot manufacture. What chemicals are there that if you put in the earth and pour some water and it will grow a big tree? These scientists, they cannot explain what is the chemical composition there. But there is. So that is in the hand of Kṛṣṇa. So this knowledge means to understand the original source. That is philosophy: find out the original source. That is knowledge. So the *vedais ca sarvair aham eva vedyo*. Actually the knowledge terminates when you understand Kṛṣṇa. He is the source of everything. So there is a

"Struggle for existence, a human race,
The only hope, His Divine Grace."

So we got this information from His Divine Grace Bhaktisiddhānta Sarasvatī Ṭhākura, and that knowledge is still going on. You are receiving through his servant. And in future the same knowledge will go to your students. This is called *paramparā* system. *Evaṁ paramparā praptam*. It is not that you have become a student, and you'll remain student. No. One day you shall become also *guru* and make more students, more students, more. That is Caitanya Mahāprahu's mission, not that perpetually, yes, one should remain perpetually a student, but he has to act as *guru*. That is the mission of Caitanya Mahāprabhu. It is not that because I am acting as *guru*, I am no longer student. No, I am still student. Caitanya Mahāprabhu taught us this instruction – that we shall always remain a foolish student before our Guru Mahārāja. That is the Vedic culture. I may be very big man, but still, I should remain a foolish student to my *guru*. That is the qualification. *Guru more mūrkha dekhi karila śāsana*. We should be always prepared to be controlled by the *guru*. That is a very good qualification. *Yasya prasādād bhagavat prasādaḥ*. And *āra nā kariha mane āśa*. So we should become always a very obedient student to our *guru*. That is the spiritual qualification.

My Guru Mahārāja wanted me to preach in the Western countries, although I was at that time an ordinary manager in a chemical firm. I never thought, but I took it seriously. So from that 1922, in 1965 it was fruitful. How many years? Forty-three years. So it is better late than never. Yes. So he desired me. I thought, "Now I am a family man. Let me adjust things." I would have accepted immediately, but I was not so intelligent at that time. I thought: my responsibility to family is there. "Let me wait." But still, Guru Mahārāja was so kind to me that when I was *gṛhastha*, I was seeing him in dreaming, and he asked me, "You come with me." So I was going, and after that I was thinking, "Oh, I will have to take *sannyāsa* and go with him?" So it appeared to me very horrible. I was not very much inclined to take *sannyāsa*, but Guru Mahārāja is so kind that he ultimately forced me to take *sannyāsa* and do this work. So it is all his kindness. So this is the memory of his kindness. So forty years ago I remember the same thing as it is in 1922, and still the same thing is going on. There is nothing new. We have nothing to do new. Simply let us present as it is. It will be successful. You see? The spirit of my writing is the same.

"Misled we are, all going astray."

This soul-killing civilization is misleading us. We must know this, this very misleading civilization. Our real aim of life is to understand our spiritual identification and search out our relationship with God, Kṛṣṇa. That is our real business. But this modern civilization is misleading us in different ways. So I wrote this, that

"Misled we are, all going astray.

Save us, lord, our fervent pray.

Wonder thy ways to turn our face,

Adore thy feet, Your Divine Grace."

So this portion he very much appreciated. So we have to find out ways how to turn the current. The current is sense enjoyment. Material life means the current is sense enjoyment, and this current has to be turned to the sense enjoyment of Kṛṣṇa. Sense enjoyment is there, but the material civilization, the misled civilization, is that the sense gratification is taken personal. When this sense gratification will be turned towards Kṛṣṇa, then our life is successful.

Just like *gopīs*. Apparently it appears that *gopīs*, they were attracted by young boy, Kṛṣṇa, and for their sense gratification they made friendship with Kṛṣṇa. No. That is not the fact. The fact is that the *gopīs* used to dress themselves nicely because by seeing them, Kṛṣṇa will be satisfied, not that for their sense gratification. Generally a girl dresses also to attract the attention of the boy. So the same thing is there, but it is Kṛṣṇa's sense gratification, not the *gopīs*'. The *gopīs* did not want anything but "Kṛṣṇa will be satisifed". That is the difference between lust and love. Love is there, only possible, when it is diverted towards Kṛṣṇa. That is love. And below that, everything is lust. So we should always remember this. The senses are not stopped, but when the gratification of the senses is directed towards Kṛṣṇa, that is *bhakti*, or love. And when the sense gratification is directed towards personal self, that is lust. This is difference beween lust and love.

So Śrīla Bhaktisiddhānta Sarasvatī Ṭhākura knew this art, how to turn our activities for the satisfaction of Kṛṣṇa. This is Kṛṣṇa consciousness movement. Therefore I wrote:

> **"Wonder thy ways to turn our face,**
> **Adore thy feet, Your Divine Grace.**
> **Forgotten Kṛṣṇa, we fallen souls,"**

Why we are fallen? Because we have forgotten. Our relationship with Kṛṣṇa is eternal. Unless it was eternal, how you Western peoples could be devotee of Kṛṣṇa? Artificially you cannot be a devotee of Kṛṣṇa. The relationship is there eternally: *nitya siddha kṛṣṇa bhakti*. By the process it is now awakened: *śravaṇādi śuddha citte karaye udaya*. It is awakened. Love between young man and young woman, it is not artificial. It is there. But by certain circumstantially, environment, the love becomes manifest. Similarly, our love for Kṛṣṇa, relationship with Kṛṣṇa, is eternal: *jīvera svarūpa haya nitya kṛṣṇa dāsa*. But we have to create such situation that eternal relation should be awakened. That is the art. That is wanted. So:

> **"Forgotten Kṛṣṇa, we fallen souls,**
> **Pay most heavy the illusion's toll."**

Because we have forgotten Kṛṣṇa we are paying heavy, heavy toll, tax, taxation. What is that taxation? The taxation is *nivartānte mṛtyu saṁsāra vartmani*. This human life is meant for understanding Kṛṣṇa, but instead of understanding Kṛṣṇa, we are understanding the so-called material science for sense gratification. This is our position. The energy which was given by nature to understand Kṛṣṇa, that is being utilized how to manufacture something for sense gratification. This is going on. This is *māyā*, illusion. Therefore it is said:

"Pay most heavy the illusion's toll."

Toll, tax. That we are paying because we have forgotten Kṛṣṇa. Therefore now we have manufactured the nuclear weapon; Russia, America, and you will have to pay heavily. They are already paying heavily. The armament preparation is going on. More than fifty per cent of the income of the state is now being spent for arms, heavily. Instead of other purposes, it is being spent for military strength, every state. So that heavy toll we are paying. And when there is war there is no limit how much we are spending for this devastation. So why? Because we have forgotten Kṛṣṇa. This is a fact.

So these people they have made the United Nations – unnecessarily fighting like dogs. So this will not solve the problems. The problem will be solved if they pass a resolution that the whole world – not only this world – Kṛṣṇa says *sarva-loka maheśvaram*. Kṛṣṇa is the proprietor, so why not accept? Actually He is the proprietor. Who has created this planet? We have created or father created? No. Kṛṣṇa has created, but we are claiming, "This portion is American, this portion is Indian, this portion is Pakistani." Unnecessary. What is the value of this claim? We may claim it for fifty or sixty or a hundred years, and after that, one kick: "Get out." Where is your claim? But they do not understand this philosophy. They are fighting, that's all. "This is mine. This is my land. This is my land." They do not know.

Kṛṣṇa said *tathā dehāntara praptiḥ*. You are American today. So tomorrow, even within America, if you become an American cow or American animal, nobody will care for you. Nobody will care for your politics. But this art they do not know. This science they do not know. They are under illusion. They are thinking that "I shall continue to remain American, so let me waste my time for American interest, so-called interest." There cannot be any interest. *Prakṛteḥ kriyamānāni guṇaiḥ karmani sarvaśaḥ.* Everything is being done by nature, and we are simply falsely thinking – *ahaṅkāra vimūḍhātmā kārtāham iti manyate.* This illusion is going on.

> **"Forgotten Kṛṣṇa, we fallen souls,**
>
> **Pay most heavy the illusion's toll."**

We are paying, paying.

> **"Darkness around, all untrace.**
>
> **The only hope, Your Divine Grace."**

This message. Simply we are in darkness. So we shall discuss later on again. Yes. So we shall discuss again. So the same thing, it is chalked out by Kṛṣṇa, and by *paramparā* system we have understood this philosophy. *Evaṁ paramparā prāptam imaṁ rājārṣayo viduḥ.* So keep this *paramparā* system. This Vyāsa-pūjā is *paramparā* system. Vyāsa-pūjā means to accept this *paramparā* system. Vyāsa. *Guru* is the representative of Vyāsa-deva because he does not change anything. What Vyāsa-deva said, your *guru* will also say the same thing. Not that "So many hundreds of thousands of years have passed away. Therefore I will give you a new formula." No. There is no new formula. The same Vyāsa-pūjā, the same philosophy. Simply we have to accept it. Then our life will be successful. Thank you very much.

Vṛndāvane

Bhajana

Vṛndāvane Bhajana

**"Worshiping the Lord in Vṛndāvana"
composed in 1958 by
His Divine Grace A. C. Bhaktivedanta Swami Prabhupāda**

INTRODUCTION

In the fall of 1958, just one year before taking *sannyāsa*, Abhay Charanaravinda Bhaktivedanta returned to his room at the Vaṁśī-Gopālajī temple in Vṛndāvana, alone and poor, after several years of traveling and preaching. He was sixty-two, but he wasn't thinking of retiring. More than ever, his mood was reflective and renounced. Since few people knew him and because he wanted to write, he kept to himself. He enjoyed deep peace as a resident of Vṛndāvana. Outside his window, the sacred Yamunā flowed by in a peaceful panorama. Without so much as leaving his room, from his doorway he could see hundreds of temples clustered together for miles in the friendly town of Vṛndāvana. The various punctual *kīrtanas* and bell-ringings in the temples, the spontaneous songs to Lord Kṛṣṇa in numerous homes and in the streets – these sounds – rose and filled the air with devotion.

On the veranda Abhay could chant *japa*, and there would be no interruption. He enjoyed a simple, almost carefree life of minimized physical wants: a few hours of rest at night, a little *prasādam* at noon, the simplest clothing. And he did not have to flatter anyone, support anyone, or manage anyone's life. His mind and intelligence were free and dwelt continually on his service to his spiritual master. He saw his present circumstances as preparation for a greater task before him. Despite his advanced age, he felt that he had barely begun his work. Yet he felt confident. He had his vision of a world association of devotees. It was not an idle dream, although he was not certain how it would all come about. But he knew his duty. For the present he would go on describing his vision, the vision of his predecessor spiritual masters, in articles and books. But as soon as possible he should go to the West. Westerners, he had concluded, were not satisfied with a materially comfortable life devoid of spiritual understanding; more than his fellow Indians, they would be open to the message of the Absolute Truth. He knew he should go. And he would go, if Lord Kṛṣṇa desired.

It was in this atmosphere that Abhay Charanaravinda composed a long Bengali poem named *Vṛndāvane Bhajana*, comprising 108 couplets divided into 27 sections. Its opening stanzas were especially self-reflective and personal, as he contemplated his realizations about material life, his temporary family, and the illusory nature of money. Then, describing the factual spiritual position of the soul and the fleeting images of bodily consciousness, Abhay pondered his memories of suffering people he had observed, who deluded themselves with an outrageous and false sense of well-being while trapped in the miserable prison house of Māyā. Next comes a section wherein Arjuna is glorified as an ideal devotee because of his proper action on behalf of Lord Kṛṣṇa, as narrated in the *Bhagavad-gītā*. Going on to philosophically challenge the neophyte devotees who do not preach to deliver others, but remain complacent in their own comfort, Abhay concluded by affirming the most important instruction he had received from his *guru:* by the power of loudly chanting the Lord's holy names, all spiritual perfection will automatically be gained by a sincere devotee.

Abhay Charanaravinda Bhaktivedanta sent this poem to his godbrother Keśava Mahārāja, who published it in the *Gauḍīya Patrikā* magazine. It appeared under the title "Poem on Vṛndāvana Worship (*Bhajana*)" in two successive issues: Volume X, Number 9 and Number 10 (November and December 1958).

Section headings

Vṛndāvane Bhajana

"Worshiping the Lord in Vṛndāvana"

SECTION 1

Lonely Realizations

vṛndāvana-dhāme āmi vase āchi ekā
e bhāvanā madhye madhye deya more dekhā

vṛndāvana-dhāme – in the transcendental abode of Vṛndāvana; *āmi* – I; *vase* – sitting;
āchi – I am; *ekā* – alone; *e* – this; *bhāvanā* – contemplation; *madhye madhye* – in the
midst; *deya* – giving; *more* – to me; *dekhā* – insights.

> I am sitting alone in the
> transcendental abode of Śrī Vṛndāvana-dhāma.
> While in this mood of contemplation,
> many realizations have been coming to me.

āche mora śtrī-putra kanyā-nāti saba
kintu artha nāi bali' biphala vaibhava

āche – there is; *mora* – my; *strī* – wife; *putra* – sons; *kanyā* – daughters; *nāti* – grandsons;
saba – all; *kintu* – but; *artha* – money; *nāi* – there is not; *bali'* – because of; *biphala* –
fruitless; *vaibhava* – opulence.

> Although I have my wife and sons,
> daughters, grandsons, everyone,
> they all consider me to be a total failure in life
> simply because I have no money.

prakṛtira nagna-rūpa dekhāle śrī-kṛṣṇa
tava kṛpā-bale āja hayechi vitṛṣṇa

prakṛtira – of the material energy; *nagna-rūpa* – the naked form; *dekhāle* – has shown; *śrī-kṛṣṇa* – Lord Kṛṣṇa; *tava* – your; *kṛpā-bale* – by the power of mercy; *āja* – today; *hayechi* – I have become; *vitṛṣṇa* – revulsion.

> O Śrī Kṛṣṇa! You have shown me
>> the naked form of material nature.
> By the power of Your mercy upon me today,
>> I have become disgusted with it all.

"yasyāham anugṛhṇāmi hariṣye tad-dhanaṁ śanaiḥ"
kṛpā-mayera ei kṛpā bujhilāma kai?

yasya – whom; *aham* – I; *anugṛhṇāmi* – I show favor; *hariṣye* – I will take away; *tat-dhanam* – his wealth; *śanaiḥ* – gradually; *kṛpā-mayera* – of He who is merciful; *ei* – this; *kṛpā* – mercy; *bujhilāma* – I have understood; *kai* – how.

> [You have stated in *Śrīmad-Bhāgavatam* (10.88.8)]:
> "I gradually take away all the wealth
>> of those to whom I show My favor."
> How can I comprehend
>> such mercy of the all-merciful Lord?

SECTION 2

A List of Names

artha-hīna dekhi' more cheḍeche sabāi
kuṭumba-ātmīya āra bandhu-jana-bhāi

artha-hīna – bereft of money; *dekhi'* – seeing; *more* – me; *cheḍeche* – have abandoned; *sabāi* – everyone; *kuṭumba* – family; *ātmīya* – relatives; *āra* – and; *bandhu-jana* – friends; *bhāi* – like brothers.

Seeing that I am penniless,
      everyone has now abandoned me —
my own family, my other relatives,
      and even my so-called friends.

duḥkha haya, hāsi pāya, ekā vasi' hāsi
māyāra saṁsāra ei kā'ke bhālavāsi?

duḥkha – unhappiness; *haya* – there is; *hāsi* – I smile; *pāya* – getting; *ekā* – alone; *vasi'* – I sit; *hāsi* – I smile; *māyāra* – of illusion; *saṁsāra* – of the material world; *ei* – this; *kā'ke* – whom; *bhālavāsi* – loved ones.

This situation is indeed miserable,
      but it simply amuses me. I sit alone and laugh.
In this mundane material world,
      who are my loved ones?

kothā gela mātā-pitā āra sneha-maya!
kothā gela jyeṣṭha yāṅrā svajanādi haya!

kothā – where; *gela* – have gone; *mātā-pitā* – my mother and father; *āra* – and; *sneha-maya* – affectionate; *kothā* – where; *gela* – have gone; *jyeṣṭha* – elders; *yāṅrā* – whom; *sva-jana-ādi* – relatives and so forth; *haya* – it is.

Where have my affectionate
      father and mother gone now?
And where are all my elders and other relatives,
      who were my own folk?

tā'dera khabara kebā debe more bala
nāma-mātra tā'dera saṁsāra raye gela

tā'dera – their; *khabara* – news; *keba* – who; *debe* – will give; *more* – to me; *bala* – please tell me; *nāma* – by name; *mātra* – only; *tā'dera* – their; *saṁsāra* – family; *raye gela* – remaining.

Who will give me news of them now,
I ask you – tell me who?
All that is left of this so-called family
is a list of names.

SECTION 3

Froth on the Seawater

samudrera phenā yena kṣaṇe sṛṣṭi-laya
māyāra saṁsāre khelā sei-bhāve haya

samudrera – of the ocean; *phenā* – foam; *yena* – just like; *kṣaṇe* – at one moment; *sṛṣṭi* – arises; *laya* – and dissolves; *māyāra* – of illusion; *saṁsāre* – in the material world; *khelā* – playing; *sei-bhāve* – in that way; *haya* – it is.

The froth upon the seawater
arises one moment and disappears the next;
the play of **māyā's** worldly illusion
is exactly like that.

keha nahe pitā-mātā ātmīya-svajana
sabā-i phenāra mata thāke alpa-kṣaṇa

keha – anybody; *nahe* – is not; *pitā-mātā* – father and mother; *ātmīya* – relative; *svajana* – family; *sabā-i* – verily everyone; *phenāra* – of sea-froth; *mata* – manner; *thāke* – remaining; *alpa-kṣaṇa* – for a brief time.

No one is actually a mother or father,
a family member or relative.
Everyone is just like the froth on the seawater,
existing for only a moment.

samudrera phenā yemana samudre miśāya
pañca-bhūtera deha tathā haye yāya laya

samudrera – of the ocean; *phenā* – foam; *yemana* – just as; *samudre* – into the ocean; *miśāya* – mixes; *pañca-bhūtera* – of five elements; *deha* – the body; *tathā* – like that; *haye yāya* – becomes; *laya* – disappears.

Just as the froth on the seawater
dissolves again into the sea,
the body made of five material elements
merges again with these elements after it dies.

kata deha ei-bhāve dharaye śarīrī
anitya śarīre mātra ātmīya tāhāri

kata – how many; *deha* – bodies; *ei-bhāve* – in this manner; *dharaye* – accepting; *śarīrī* – the embodied soul; *anitya* – temporary; *śarīre* – to the body; *mātra* – only; *ātmīya* – relatives; *tāhāri* – their.

How many fleeting forms does the
embodied soul take in this manner?
His so-called family members are only related
to this temporary external body.

SECTION 4

Eternal Spiritual Relatives

ātmīya sabā-i bhāi! ātmāra sambandhe
ātmīyatā nāhi haya māyā-maya gandhe

ātmīya – family members; *sabā-i* – verily all; *bhāi* – O brothers; *ātmāra* – of the spirit soul; *sambandhe* – in relationship; *ātmīyatā* – kinship; *nāhi haya* – it is not; *māyā-maya* – illusory; *gandhe* – tinged.

> **O brothers! All of us are actually relatives,**
>> **but only on the platform of pure spirit soul.**
> **These eternal relationships are not tinged**
>> **with the temporary delusions of *māyā*.**

sakalera ātmā yini svayaṁ bhagavān
tāṅhāra sambandhe viśve sabā-i samāna

sakalera – of everyone; *ātmā* – spirit; *yini* – who; *svayam bhagavān* – the Supreme Lord Himself; *tāṅhāra* – His; *sambandhe* – in relationship; *viśve* – in the universe; *sabā-i* – verily all; *samāna* – the same.

> **The Supreme Lord is Himself**
>> **the ultimate Soul of everyone.**
> **In their eternal relation to Him,**
>> **all souls in the universe are equal.**

ātmīya tomāra bhāi! yata jīva-koṭi
kṛṣṇera sambandhe tāṅrā haya paripāṭi

ātmīya – family; *tomāra* – your; *bhāi* – O brothers; *yata* – whichever; *jīva-koṭi* – tens of millions of spirit souls; *kṛṣṇera* – of Kṛṣṇa; *sambandhe* – in relationship; *tāṅrā* – their; *haya* – is; *paripāṭi* – orderly arrangement.

> **O brothers! All the millions of spirit souls**
>> **are your personal relatives.**
> **In their true relationship with Kṛṣṇa,**
>> **they all co-exist in complete harmony.**

"kṛṣṇa bhuli sei jīva" bhoga-vāñchā kare
māyāra saṁsāra tāi jāpaṭiyā dhare

kṛṣṇa – Lord Kṛṣṇa; *bhuli* – forgetting; *sei* – that; *jīva* – soul; *bhoga-vāñchā* – desirous of enjoyment; *kare* – does; *māyāra* – of illusion; *saṁsāra* – material world; *tāi* – for that; *jāpaṭiyā* – clasping; *dhare* – holds.

"Forgetting Kṛṣṇa, the living entity desires
personal enjoyment separate from Him." [*Cc. Madhya* 20.117]
Thus the spirit soul enters the temporary material world
and falls into the powerful clutches of *māyā*.

SECTION 5

Fallen Souls Suffer

karma-phale āse saba nānā veśa dhari'
veśete majiyā thāke bhuliyā śrī-hari

karma-phale – by the results of fruitive reactions; *āse* – coming; *saba* – all; *nānā* –
various; *veśa* – dresses; *dhari'* – accepting; *veśete* – in the dress; *majiyā* – immersing;
thāke – remains; *bhuliyā* – forgetting; *śrī-hari* – Lord Hari.

As a result of accumulated fruitive reactions,
all the fallen souls accept various bodily forms.
Becoming engrossed in these material disguises,
they completely forget about their Lord, Śrī Hari.

ataeva māyā tāre deya bahu duḥkha
duḥkhe hābu-ḍubu tabu tāhe māne sukha

ataeva – therefore; *māyā* – illusion; *tāre* – to them; *deya* – gives; *bahu* – great; *duḥkha*
– misery; *duḥkhe* – in misery; *hābu-ḍubu* – surfacing and submerging; *tabu* – then; *tāhe*
– by that; *māne* – considers to be; *sukha* – happiness.

Therefore *māyā* provides the embodied souls
with a great variety of material miseries.
But as they rise and sink in the wretched waves of suffering,
they still imagine this experience to be enjoyment.

cira-rogī duḥkha-bhogī śayyāte śuiyā
"bhālo āchi āja" kahe hāsiyā hāsiyā

cira-rogī – chronically ill; *duḥkha-bhogī* – one who is suffering great misery; *śayyāte* – upon the bed; *śuiyā* – lying; *bhālo* – very well; *āchi* – I am; *āja* – today; *kahe* – he says; *hāsiyā hāsiyā* – smiling and laughing.

A chronically ill patient lies upon his bed,
  miserably suffering intense pain,
but he smiles and laughs as he tells his visitors,
  "Today I am doing fine!"

hāsi pāya tāra "bhālo thākāra" kathāya
māyā-baddha-jīvera bhālo ei-bhāve haya

hāsi pāya – I get a laugh; *tāra* – his; *bhālo thākāra* – of "doing fine"; *kathāya* – by the talk; *māyā-baddha* – bound by illusion; *jīvera* – of the soul; *bhālo* – fine; *ei-bhāve* – in this manner; *haya* – it is.

All his talk about "doing fine"
  really makes me laugh aloud.
This is the "fine" of the spirit soul
  who is totally bound up in *māyā's* gross illusion.

SECTION 6

Plans for "Doing Fine"

kata "plyāna" kare tārā bhālo thākibāre
prakṛti bhāṅgiyā deya saba bāre bāre

kata – how many; *plyāna* – so-called plans; *kare* – making; *tārā* – their; *bhālo thākibāre* – for doing fine; *prakṛti* – material nature; *bhāṅgiyā* – breaking; *deya* – gives; *saba* – everything; *bāre bāre* – again and again.

They make a great many plans
    to live comfortably in this world, "doing fine."
But material nature smashes all of their arrangements
    one after the other.

"daivī hy eṣā guṇa-mayī" bhagavānera māyā
"bhālo thākāra" artha bujha bhālo ka're bhāyā

daivī – transcendental; *hi* – certainly; *eṣā* – this; *guṇa-mayī* – consisting of the three
modes of material nature; *bhagavānera* – of the Lord; *māyā* – illusion; *bhālo thākāra* – for
doing fine; *artha* – the meaning; *bujha* – please understand; *bhālo* – well; *ka're* – doing;
bhāyā – O brothers.

The Lord's **māyā** is "divine energy, consisting of
    the three modes of material nature." [Bg. 7.14]
O brothers! Please try to understand the reality
    of this illusion of supposedly "doing fine."

keha "bhālo" nāi hethā "tabu bhālo" bale
ei-bhāve māyā saba baddha-jīve chale

keha – anyone; *bhālo* – fine; *nāi* – is not; *hethā* – here; *tabu* – still; *bhālo* – fine; *bale* – he
says; *ei-bhāve* – in this way; *māyā* – illusion; *saba* – all; *baddha-jīve* – to the bound souls;
chale – cheats.

Although no one is actually fine here in this world,
    one persists in saying, "I am fine!"
In this way, **māyā** completely deceives
    the conditioned souls within her grasp.

chalanāya bhuli jīva sarvadā majgula
māyā lāgi mare tabu bhāṅge nāko bhula

chalanāya – by that cheating; *bhuli* – forgetting; *jīva* – souls; *sarvadā* – always; *majgula*
– engrossed; *māyā* – illusion; *lāgi* – because of; *mare* – kicking; *tabu* – still; *bhāṅge* –
breaking; *nāko* – does not; *bhula* – forgetfulness.

Being enchanted by *māyā's* deception,

these souls remain perpetually engrossed in illusion.
Although *māyā* severely kicks them during their attempts to enjoy,
they still refuse to give up their enchantment.

SECTION 7

The Gift of *Bhakti*

bāra bāra "plyāna" kari bāra bāra bhāṅge
kakhana bhumite paḍi' kakhana ta' paṅke

bāra bāra – again and again; *plyāna* – plans; *kari* – making; *bāra bāra* – repeatedly;
bhāṅge – foiling; *kakhana* – sometimes; *bhumite* – on the ground; *paḍi'* – falling down;
kakhana – sometimes; *ta'* – indeed; *paṅke* – in the mud.

Again and again they make their plans,

which again and again are thwarted.
Sometimes they fall upon the hard dry earth,

and sometimes they fall in the soft wet mud.

ei-rūpa brahmāṇḍa-bhari' (jīva) karaye bhramaṇa
guru-kṛṣṇa-kṛpāya pāya bhakti nitya-dhana

ei-rūpa – in this way; *brahmā-aṇḍa* – the egglike-shaped material universes of Brahmā;
bhari' – filling; *jīva* – the souls; *karaye* – doing; *bhramaṇa* – wandering; *guru-kṛṣṇa* – of
the spiritual master and Kṛṣṇa; *kṛpāya* – by the mercy; *pāya* – they receive; *bhakti* – of
devotional service; *nitya-dhana* – the eternal treasure.

In this way the fallen souls

wander throughout the egglike material universe
until, eventually, by the causeless mercy of *guru* and Kṛṣṇa,

they receive the eternal treasure of devotional service.

sei dhana mile yadi āra dhana chāḍe
anāyāse ca'le yāya saṁsārera pāre

sei – that; *dhana* – treasure; *mile* – getting; *yadi* – if; *āra* – other; *dhana* – treasure; *chāḍe* – abandoning; *anāyāse* – easily; *ca'le yāya* – goes; *saṁsārera pāre* – beyond the material world of birth and death.

Upon receiving that divine treasure of *bhakti*,
 if they reject all mundane ideas of treasure,
they can very easily travel beyond
 the temporary material sphere.

bhava-pāre āche cid-vaicitrya apāra
nitya-śānti-nitya-sukhe karaye vihāra

bhava-pāre – beyond matter; *āche* – there is; *cit-vaicitrya* – variegatedness of pure consciousness; *apāra* – limitless; *nitya* – eternal; *śānti* – peace; *nitya* – eternal; *sukhe* – in bliss; *karaye* – does; *vihāra* – sport.

Beyond the limited world of dull matter
 exist spiritual wonders in limitless variety.
Everyone living there is truly enjoying
 eternal peace and everlasting happiness.

SECTION 8

Relishing Transcendental Mellows

bātula kahaye – "sethā saba nirākāra
nirviśeṣa tini yena śūnyera prakāra"

bātula – a madman; *kahaye* – says; *sethā* – there [in the spiritual world]; *saba* – everything; *nirākāra* – is formless; *nirviśeṣa* – without attributes; *tini* – He; *yena* – just as; *śunyera* – of the void; *prakāra* – variety.

Only a madman ignorantly declares,

"Everything in the spiritual world is formless.

God has no personal qualities,

for ultimately there is only a limitless void."

rasera bhāṇḍārī tini – "raso vai saḥ"

rasika bhāvuka seve hai tāṅra vaśa

rasera – of transcendental mellows; *bhāṇḍārī* – the storehouse; *tini* – He; *rasaḥ* – mellow; *vai* – verily; *saḥ* – He; *rasika* – relisher; *bhāvuka* – emotional devotee; *seve* – renders service; *hai* – does; *tāṅra* – of His; *vaśa* – subservience.

God is the storehouse of transcendental mellows:

"Verily He is *rasa* itself." [*Taittirīya Upaniṣad* 2.7.1]

The intelligent devotees who ecstatically relish His mellows

render service to Him in submission.

śānta, dāsya, sakhya, vātsalya rasa āra

sarva-rasa-śreṣṭha mādhurya rasa sāra

śānta – neutrality; *dāsya* – servitude; *sakhya* – friendship; *vātsalya* – parental; *rasa* – mellow; *āra* – and; *sarva-rasa* – of all mellows; *śreṣṭha* – the best; *mādhurya* – conjugal love; *rasa* – mellow; *sāra* – the essence.

They serve Him in the mellows of neutrality,

servitude, friendship, parental affection,

and in the *rasa* that is the finest of all,

the quintessential conjugal mellow.

cid-jagate "rasa" saba haya upādeya

māyāte tāra chāyā-mātra kintu saba heya

cit-jagate – in the spiritual world; *rasa* – mellow; *saba* – all; *haya* – is; *upādeya* – tasteful; *māyāte* – in the material realm; *tāra* – those; *chāyā-mātra* – only a reflection; *kintu* – but; *saba* – all; *heya* – despicable.

When expressed within the spiritual world,

all of these mellows are thoroughly relishable,

but in the material world, being only distorted reflections,
these mellows all become repulsive.

SECTION 9

The Wise vs. the Poor

kṛṣṇa yei bhaje sei hayata' catura
māyā yei bhaje sei hayata' "phatura"

kṛṣṇa – Lord Kṛṣṇa; *yei* – whoever; *bhaje* – worships; *sei* – he; *hayata'* – becomes; *catura* – wise; *māyā* – illusion; *yei* – whoever; *bhaje* – worships; *sei* – he; *hayata'* – becomes; *phatura* – poverty-stricken.

> **Whoever worships Kṛṣṇa in devotion**
> **is truly wise;**
> **Whoever worships *māyā* in illusion**
> **is truly poor.**

"phatura" haibāra lāgi anitya vilāsa
sambandha-jñāna-hīnera haya karma-bandha phāṅsa

phatura – poverty-stricken; *haibāra* – to become; *lāgi* – on account of; *anitya* – temporary; *vilāsa* – enjoyment; *sambandha-jñāna* – knowledge of the relationship to Kṛṣṇa; *hīnera* – of one who is bereft; *haya* – there is; *karma-bandha* – bound by fruitive reactions; *phāṅsa* – the noose.

> **Attempting to enjoy fleeting fantasies,**
> **the fallen soul thereby becomes destitute.**
> **Bereft of the knowledge of his eternal relationship with Kṛṣṇa,**
> **he is ensnared in the noose of his own fruitive reactions.**

arjuna karaye yuddha (āra) duryodhana kare
arjuna bhakta-śreṣṭha duryodhana mare

arjuna – Arjuna; *karaye* – does; *yuddha* – fight; *āra* – and; *duryodhana* – Duryodhana; *kare* – does the same; *arjuna* – Arjuna; *bhakta-śreṣṭha* – the best of devotees; *duryodhana* – Duryodhana; *mare* – dies.

> **Arjuna fought in the ancient Battle of Kurukṣetra,**
>> **and Duryodhana also fought in the same battle.**
> **Arjuna was the best of devotees,**
>> **whereas Duryodhana simply perished.**

> *eka yuddha-kṣetre dui priyāpriya haya*
> *buddhimāna loka yei bujhite pāraya*

eka – the same; *yuddha-kṣetre* – on the battlefield; *dui* – two; *priya-apriya* – dear and not dear; *haya* – there is; *buddhimāna* – intelligent; *loka* – people; *yei* – who; *bujhite* – to understand; *pāraya* – are able.

> **These two, though on the same battlefield, were different:**
>> **one was a friend of Kṛṣṇa, the other a foe.**
> **Persons who possess intelligence**
>> **can clearly understand the difference.**

SECTION 10

Understand and Fight

> *"sambandha" jāniyā yebā jīvana-yuddha kare*
> *seita' vāñciyā thāke āra saba mare*

sambandha – relationship; *jāniyā* – knowing; *yebā* – whoever; *jīvana-yuddha* – the fight for survival; *kare* – does; *seita'* – this indeed; *vāñciyā thāke* – survive; *āra* – others; *saba* – all; *mare* – die.

Whoever knows the spirit soul's
    eternal relationship with Lord Kṛṣṇa
and fights the battle of life for His sake
    will survive, while all others will die.

"sambandha" nā jāni' yebā āna pathe dhāya
kṛṣṇa-prīti nāhi mile vṛthā janma yāya

sambandha – relationship; *nā* – not; *jāni'* – knowing; *yebā* – whoever; *āna* – another; *pathe* – on the path; *dhāya* – runs; *kṛṣṇa-prīti* – love for Kṛṣṇa; *nāhi* – not; *mile* – receiving; *vṛthā* – useless; *janma* – birth; *yāya* – passes.

Whoever does not know this relationship with Kṛṣṇa
    and foolishly runs down another path
will never attain love for Kṛṣṇa,
    but simply waste his entire life.

kṛṣṇa se "sambandha" ādi bhālo kare bujha
se-"sambandha" rākhi' tumi māyā sāthe yujha

kṛṣṇa – Kṛṣṇa; *se* – that; *sambandha* – relationship; *ādi* – and so forth [*abhideya* and *prayojana*]; *bhalo* – nicely; *kare* – does; *bujha* – please understand; *se* – that, *sambandha* – relationship; *rākhi'* – keeping; *tumi* – you; *māyā* – illusion; *sāthe* – with; *yujha* – please fight.

First properly understand your relationship with Kṛṣṇa,
    your duties in relation to Him (**abhideya**),
    and the ultimate goal of ecstatic love for Him (**prayojana**).
Then, remaining firmly fixed in your alliance with Kṛṣṇa,
    go and confidently fight the battle against *māyā*.

tāhā chāḍi' haya yebā jñāna-karma-vīra
mokṣa nāhi pāya tārā haya ta' asthira

tāhā – that; *chāḍi'* – abandoning; *haya* – there is; *yebā* – whoever; *jñāna-karma* – knowledge and action; *vīra* – valorous; *mokṣa* – liberation; *nāhi* – does not; *pāya* – get; *tārā* – their; *haya* – is; *ta'* – indeed; *asthira* – restless.

Those who abandon their devotional relationship with the Lord
    and try to become powerful
    within the realms of intellectual knowledge (*jñāna-yoga*)
    and fruitive action (***karma-yoga***)
Never attain liberation from the material world
    but simply remain disturbed throughout their lives.

SECTION 11

Senses Uncontrollable by Yoga

name-mātrā mahādhīra, sakale aśānta
bhukti-mukti-siddhi-kāmīra indriya adānta

nāme – in name; *mātrā* – only; *mahā-dhīra* – a great sober person; *sakale* – always; *aśānta* – agitated; *bhukti-mukti-siddhi* – sense enjoyment, liberation, and mystic perfection; *kāmīra* – of one who is desirous; *indriya* – the senses; *adānta* – uncontrolled.

In name only, **yogīs** appear to be eminent and grave personalities,
    but actually they are constantly agitated by **māyā**.
Hankering after material enjoyment, liberation, and mystic perfection,
    they are sensually uncontrolled.

adānta indriya nahe yoga-bale vaśa
kata muni yogī saba hayeche vivaśa

adānta – unrestrained; *indriya* – senses; *nahe* – are not; *yoga-bale* – by the power of performing *haṭha-yoga*; *vaśa* – subdued; *kata* – how many; *muni* – sages; *yogī* – and *yogīs*; *saba* – all; *hayeche* – there are; *vivaśa* – out of control.

Unrestrained senses can never be subdued
    even by the power of diligent *yoga* practice.
How many great *munis* and *yogīs* in the past
    have all been overwhelmed by sensual urges?

hṛṣīkeśa-sevā vinā hṛṣīka-damana
karamera phera saba bhuñjāya śamana

hṛṣīka-īśa – the Lord, master of the senses; *sevā* – the service; *vinā* – without; *hṛṣīka-damana* – control of the senses; *karamera* – of fruitive reactions; *phera* – reverse; *saba* – everyone; *bhuñjāya* – suffering; *śamana* – Yama, god of death.

Without serving Lord Hṛṣīkeśa, master of the senses,
    they manage to subdue the senses only for a time.
Eventually they return to fruitive material activities
    and then suffer under Yamarāja, the god of death.

yogete indriya-saṁyama kabhu nāhi haya
āgama-purāṇe tāhā bhuri-bhuri kaya

yogete – by performance of *yoga*; *indriya-saṁyama* – restraint of the senses; *kabhu nāhi* – never; *haya* – it is; *āgama-purāṇe* – in the *āgama* scriptures and *Purāṇa* histories; *tāhā* – that; *bhuri-bhuri* – in many places; *kaya* – is narrated.

The senses can never be permanently restrained
    by performing physical *yoga* exercises.
This is clearly explained in many places
    throughout the *Āgama* and *Purāṇa* scriptures.

SECTION 12

No Success without Kṛṣṇa

yogīra āsane vasechila viśvāmitra
janma dila śakuntalā sundarī pavitra

yogīra – of an ascetic; *āsane* – upon the seat; *vasechila* – was sitting; *viśvāmitra* – the sage named Viśvāmitra; *janma* – birth; *dila* – gave; *śakuntalā* – named Śakuntalā; *sundarī* – the beautiful girl; *pavitra* – very pure.

Although the great sage Viśvāmitra
  was sitting and meditating in mystic trance,
he still fell down from that *yoga* practice to unite with Menakā
  and begot a beautiful, pure daughter named Śakuntalā.

ei-bhāve yoga-bhraṣṭa jñānīra ki kathā
karmī saba mūḍha-jana vyathita sarvathā

ei-bhāve – in this way; *yoga-bhraṣṭa* – unsuccessful in *yoga* practice; *jñānīra* – of the knowledge seeker; *ki kathā* – what can be said; *karmī* – fruitive workers; *saba* – all; *mūḍha-jana* – foolish persons; *vyathita* – afflicted; *sarvathā* – always.

In this way the unsuccessful *yogīs* fall down,
  and what to speak of the intellectual *jñānīs*?
As for the common *karmīs*, grossly foolish like asses,
  they are perpetually afflicted with suffering.

kṛṣṇa yāre kṛpā kari' upadeśa dena
tini ta' arjuna-sama bhāgyavān hana

kṛṣṇa – Lord Kṛṣṇa; *yāre* – to whom; *kṛpā kari'* – showing mercy; *upadeśa* – instructions; *dena* – giving; *tini* – he; *ta'* – indeed; *arjuna-sama* – just like Arjuna; *bhāgyavān* – fortunate; *hana* – becomes.

Those to whom Lord Kṛṣṇa shows His mercy
  by personally giving instruction,
become equally as fortunate
  as the great devotee Arjuna.

āpanāra sukha-lāgi yebā yuddha kare
duryodhanera mata se savaṁśete mare

āpanāra – one's own; *sukha-lāgi* – for the purpose of pleasure; *yebā* – whoever; *yuddha kare* – fights; *duryodhanera* – of Duryodhana; *mata* – the same way; *se* – he; *sa-vaṁśete* – along with his dynasty; *mare* – dies.

But whoever fights the battle of life
for the sake of his own selfish pleasure
dies, along with his entire dynasty,
just like the foolish demon Duryodhana.

SECTION 13

The Message of the *Bhagavad-gītā*

kṛṣṇera lāgiyā yebā nitya yuddha kare
ṛddhi, siddhi, jñāna tāra muṣṭira bhitare

kṛṣṇera – of Kṛṣṇa; *lāgiyā* – on behalf of; *yebā* – whoever; *nitya* – perpetually; *yuddha kare* – fights; *ṛddhi* – prosperity; *siddhi* – mystic perfection; *jñāna* – knowledge; *tāra* – his; *muṣṭira* – of the fist; *bhitare* – within.

Whoever daily fights the battle of life
only for Lord Kṛṣṇa's sake discovers prosperity,
mystic perfection, and transcendental knowledge
in the palm of his hand.

gītāra upadeśa bhai bujha bhālo kari
pāibe kṛṣṇera sevā bhajibe śrī-hari

gītāra – of the *Bhagavad-gītā*; *upadeśa* – the instructions; *bhāi* – O brothers; *bujha* – please understand; *bhālo kari* – very thoroughly; *pāibe* – it will be attained; *kṛṣṇera* – of Kṛṣṇa; *sevā* – the service; *bhajibe* – and will worship; *śrī-hari* – Lord Hari.

> **O brothers! Take care to properly understand**
> **the transcendental message of the *Bhagavad-gītā*.**
> **Then you will attain Lord Kṛṣṇa's service**
> **and remain ever engaged in the worship of Śrī Hari.**

> *sarva-guṇe su-sampanna bhakta-jana haya*
> *"ahiṁsā" "akrodha" tāṅra kāche kichu naya*

sarva-guṇe – with all good attributes; *su-sampanna* – nicely endowed; *bhakta-jana* – the devotees; *haya* – they are; *ahiṁsā* – nonviolence; *akrodha* – not angry; *tāṅra* – their; *kāche* – in possession of; *kichu* – something; *naya* – nothing.

> **The Lord's devotees are richly endowed**
> **with all transcendental qualities.**
> **They hold no artificial worldly concepts such as**
> ***ahiṁsa*, nonviolence, and *akrodha*, freedom from anger.**

> *bhakta-dvāre jīve śikṣā dibena śrī-hari*
> *tāhāra sahāya haila "pārtha"-nāma-dhārī*

bhakta-dvāre – by the devotees; *jīve* – to the fallen souls; *śikṣā* – instructions; *dibena* – will give; *śrī-hari* – Lord Hari; *tāhāra* – their; *sahāya* – helper; *haila* – became; *pārtha* – the son of Pṛthā [Arjuna]; *nāma-dhārī* – bearing the name.

> **Using His devotees as instruments,**
> **Śrī Hari gives instructions to the fallen souls.**
> **One such assistant of His is known as Pārtha,**
> **the son of mother Pṛthā.**

SECTION 14

Arjuna Surrenders to Kṛṣṇa

sājila arjuna yena māyā-baddha nara
mohitera nyāya haila pāṇḍava-sodara

sājila – played the part of; *arjuna* – Arjuna; *yena* – just as; *māyā-baddha* – bound by illusion; *nara* – human being; *mohitera* – of a bewildered soul; *nyāya* – like; *haila* – had become; *pāṇḍava-sodara* – the brother of the Pāṇḍavas [Arjuna].

Arjuna had taken himself to be
a conditioned soul bound by *māyā*.
Thus the brother of the Pāṇḍavas
behaved like one bewildered.

ātmīya-svajana-hiṁsā, pare rājya-bhoga
ithe kibā sukha – pārtha dekhāilā śoka

ātmīya – relatives; *sva-jana* – family; *hiṁsā* – slaughter; *pare* – afterwards; *rājya-bhoga* – enjoying the kingdom; *ithe* – by doing this; *kibā sukha* – what happiness; *pārtha* – Arjuna; *dekhāilā* – expressed; *śoka* – lamentation.

Arjuna expressed his lamentation thus:
"Killing my family members and relatives
and afterward enjoying rulership of their kingdom –
what kind of happiness will that bring me?"

sei ta' "dehātma-buddhi" ātmīya-jñāna ka're
kṣatriya haiyā snehe yuddha-kṣetra chāḍe

sei ta' – all that; *deha-ātma* – the body as the self; *buddhi* – the mentality; *ātmīya-jñāna* – conception of kinsmanship; *ka're* – accepts; *kṣatriya* – a warrior; *haiyā* – being; *snehe* – in personal affection; *yuddha-kṣetra* – the battlefield; *chāḍe* – abandons.

Thus he displayed illusory bodily consciousness
by imagining the bodies of others to be his kinsmen.

**Although he was a trained warrior, he left the battlefield
out of sentimental affection for family members.**

*moha dekhi' kṛṣṇa tā'ra karila nindana
ataeva arjuna kaila śiṣyatva grahaṇa*

moha – bewilderment; *dekhi'* – seeing; *kṛṣṇa* – Lord Kṛṣṇa; *tā'ra* – his; *karila* – had done; *nindana* – chastisement; *ataeva* – therefore; *arjuna* – Arjuna; *kaila* – did; *śiṣyatva* – discipleship; *grahaṇa* – acceptance.

**Seeing Arjuna's cowardly bewilderment,
Lord Kṛṣṇa personally chastised him.
Thereafter Arjuna surrendered to Kṛṣṇa
and became His disciple.**

SECTION 15

The *Bhagavad-gītā* Destroys Internal Bondage

*śiṣya haiyā kare yei gītāra śravaṇa
ghucibe ajñāna āra saṁsāra-bandhana*

śiṣya haiyā – becoming a disciple; *kare* – doing; *yei* – which; *gītāra śravaṇa* – hearing the Bhagavad-gītā; *ghucibe* – will be dispelled; *ajñāna* – ignorance; *āra* – and; *saṁsāra-bandhana* – bondage to the material world.

**As Kṛṣṇa's disciple, Arjuna listened
to the Lord's recitation of the *Bhagavad-gītā*,
hearing which surely destroys
all ignorance and material bondage.**

*saṁsāra ghucila kintu bāhya-nyāsī naya
gītāra tātparye gṛhī e-rūpa bujhāya*

saṁsāra – material bondage; *ghucila* – having been dispelled; *kintu* – but; *bāhya-nyāsī* – externally renouncing; *naya* – not; *gītāra* – of the Gītā; *tātparye* – in the meaning; *gṛhī* – householders; *e-rūpa* – in this way; *bujhāya* – is understood.

> Although Arjuna's material bondage was destroyed,
>> he never renounced the external world, as a *sannyāsī* does.
> Following his example, those who are householders
>> can understand the true message of the *Bhagavad-gītā*.

> *"kariṣye vacanaṁ tava" sei mantra-siddhi*
> *ataeva yuddhe tāṅ'ra ha'la yaśo-vṛddhi*

kariṣye – I shall execute; *vacanam* – order; *tava* – Your; *sei* – that; *mantra-siddhi* – perfection of sound formulas; *ataeva* – therefore; *yuddhe* – by fighting; *tāṅ'ra* – his; *ha'la* – had become; *yaśo-vṛddhi* – spreading of his fame.

> "I am now firm and free from doubt and am prepared
>> to act according to Your instructions." [*Bg.* 18.73]
> Arjuna spoke this most perfect of *mantras*
>> and thus fought that battle and became forever famous.

> *vaiṣṇava nirīha saba mālā japa kare*
> *e kon vaiṣṇava arjuna saṁsāra-bhitare?*

vaiṣṇava – a devotee; *nirīha* – gentle; *saba* – all; *mālā* – on beads; *japa kare* – chants holy names; *e* – this; *kon* – how; *vaiṣṇava* – devotee; *arjuna* – like Arjuna; *saṁsāra-bhitare* – in the midst of the world.

> "The Vaiṣṇava devotees of the Lord
>> are typically nonviolent and indifferent to the world;
>> they simply chant holy names on their *japa* beads.
> How, then, can Arjuna,
>> a warrior in the midst of worldly activity,
>> be considered a devotee?" [someone may ask.]

SECTION 16

True Nature of a Devotee

"nirdvandva vaiṣṇava śudhu japa kare mālā"
balaye ei-rūpa yā'rā khāya mana-kolā

nirdvandva – peaceful; *vaiṣṇava* – a devotee; *śudhu* – simply; *japa kare* – chants; *mālā* – on beads; *balaye* – saying; *ei-rūpa* – in this manner; *yā'rā* – whose; *khāya* – eats; *mana-kolā* – mentally-concocted bananas.

"A Vaiṣṇava is completely peaceful
**   and simply spends his time chanting *japa* on his beads" –**
whoever speaks in this way only eats the mind's bananas!
**   [He reaches a false conclusion based on external appearances.]**

vaiṣṇava nirīha, akṛta-droha, haya ta' svabhāve
kintu nahe hīna-vīrya yathā loka bhāve

vaiṣṇava – a devotee; *nirīha* – harmless; *akṛta-droha* – showing no malice; *haya ta'* – being; *svabhāve* – naturally; *kintu* – but; *nahe* – not; *hīna-vīrya* – without valor; *yathā* – just as; *loka* – the general public; *bhāve* – thinking.

A devotee of the Lord is naturally gentle in disposition
**   and bears no malice toward other living beings.**
But that does not mean he is a weakling and possesses no valor,
**   as many people foolishly think.**

bhāratera dui yuddhe dui mahāśaya
vaiṣṇavera agraṇī tārā karila vijaya

bhāratera – of India; *dui yuddhe* – in the two battles [described in the *Rāmāyaṇa* and *Mahābhārata*]; *dui mahāśaya* – two great souls [Hanumān and Arjuna]; *vaiṣṇavera* – of the devotee; *agraṇī* – foremost; *tārā* – they; *karila* – have done; *vijaya* – conquest.

In the two great battles of ancient India,
**   there were two great heroes.**
Both were exalted devotees of the Lord,
**   and thus they were victorious.**

nijendriya tṛpti-vāñchāya yuddha nāhi kare
vaiṣṇava baliyā tāi vidita saṁsāre

nija-indriya – one's own senses; *tṛpti* – satisfaction; *vāñchāya* – being desirous; *yuddha* – fight; *nāhi* – not; *kare* – doing; *vaiṣṇava* – a devotee; *baliyā* – because; *tāi* – just so; *vidita* – is known; *saṁsāre* – throughout the world.

It is known throughout the entire world
that one who is a Vaiṣṇava
never fights a battle out of desires
for personal sense gratification.

SECTION 17

A Vaiṣṇava is not Inactive

vaiṣṇava nā dekhiyā bale vaiṣṇava niṣkriya
vaiṣṇava "prabhura" sevāya sadā-i sakriya

vaiṣṇava – a devotee; *nā dekhiyā* – not seeing; *bale* – one says; *vaiṣṇava* – a devotee; *niṣkriya* – is without actions; *vaiṣṇava* – a devotee; *prabhura sevāya* – in service of the Lord; *sadā-i* – indeed always; *sakriya* – acting.

Those who have never seen a true Vaiṣṇava
mistakenly claim that a Vaiṣṇava is inactive.
Actually, a Vaiṣṇava is always active,
but only in the Supreme Lord's devotional service.

prāṇa-hīna kaniṣṭha sei sevā nāhi kare
pratiṣṭhāra tare thāke nirjanera ghare

prāṇa-hīna – bereft of life; *kaniṣṭha* – the neophyte; *sei* – he; *sevā* – service; *nāhi kare* – does not do; *pratiṣṭhāra* – of reputation; *tare* – on account of; *thāke* – resides; *nirjanera* – of solitary; *ghare* – in a cottage.

> The neophyte devotee, being bereft of true life,
>> does not engage in such active devotional service to the Lord.
> Hoping to earn the reputation of a so-called sage,
>> he pretentiously retires to a secluded cottage.

> *vaiṣṇava-praṇamya śrīla nityānanda rāya*
> *māra khāya, prema deya yathāya tathāya*

vaiṣṇava-praṇamya – worshipable for the devotees; *śrīla* – the splendrous; *nityānanda rāya* – Lord Nityānanda; *māra khāya* – being struck; *prema deya* – bestowing ecstatic love; *yathāya tathāya* – everywhere.

> Śrīla Nityānanda Rāya is worshipable by all devotees
>> because even when He was physically attacked
> by the degraded souls Jagāi and Mādhāi,
>> He simply bestowed upon them ecstatic love of God.

> *cakra-pāṇi gaura-hari sethā karila śāsana*
> *vaiṣṇava-vidveṣī tabe haila damana*

cakra-pāṇi – wielding the Sudarśana disk; *gaura-hari* – Lord Caitanya; *sethā* – there; *karila* – had attempted; *śāsana* – punishment; *vaiṣṇava-vidveṣī* – those envious of the devotees; *tabe* – then; *haila* – became; *damana* – subdued.

> Lord Gaurahari had angrily raised His Sudarśana disk
>> to kill those envious offenders of the Vaiṣṇavas,
> but by Lord Nityānanda's mercy
>> they were transformed into Vaiṣṇavas.

SECTION 18

Vaiṣṇavas Actively Show Mercy

āpani ācari' "prabhu" jīvere śikhāya
āpana vañcaka yei sei nirjane bhajāya

āpani – Himself; *ācari'* – showing the example; *prabhu* – the Lord; *jīvere* – unto the fallen souls; *śikhāya* – instructing; *āpana* – oneself; *vañcaka* – cheater; *yei* – who; *sei* – he; *nirjane* – in solitude; *bhajāya* – worships.

Showing the ideal example Himself,
Lord Caitanya engaged in preaching to the fallen souls.
Those who attempt to worship Him in a solitary place
verily cheat themselves.

jagat bhariyā gela jagāi-mādhāiye
nityānanda-vaṁśa bāḍāya śiṣya-sampradāye

jagat – the universe; *bhariyā* – filling up; *gela* – has gone; *jagāi-mādhāiye* – with Jagāis and Mādhāis; *nityānanda* – Lord Nityānanda; *vaṁśa* – the lineage; *bāḍāya* – increasing; *śiṣya-sampradāye* – in the disciplic succession of their followers.

The whole world has now filled up
with countless Jagāis and Mādhāis needing deliverance,
but many in the lineage of Lord Nityānanda
are simply busy increasing the number of their disciples.

khāya dāya thāke beśa ha'ye cintā-hīna
vaiṣṇavera ucita nahe thākā dayā-hīna

khāya dāya – eating and sleeping; *thāke* – living; *beśa* – nicely; *ha'ye* – being; *cintā-hīna* – carefree; *vaiṣṇavera* – of the devotee; *ucita* – befitting; *nahe* – is not; *thākā* – to remain; *dayā-hīna* – without showing mercy.

Eating and sleeping nicely, enjoying the good life,
they remain free from personal inconvenience.

But for a true Vaiṣṇava it is unacceptable to live
without actively showing mercy to fallen souls.

"mādhurya kādambinī"-grantha cakravartī gāya
siddhānta dekhaha tathā kibā tān'ra "rāya"

mādhurya kādambinī – named *Mādhurya Kādambinī* (*The Cloudbank of Sweetness*);
grantha – the book; *cakravartī* – Śrīla Viśvanātha Cakravartī; *gāya* – sings; *siddhānta* –
conclusion; *dekhaha* – just see; *tathā* – that; *kibā* – what is; *tān'ra* – his; *rāya* – verdict.

In his wonderful book ***Mādhurya-Kādambinī*** [1.3],
Śrīla Viśvanātha Cakravartī Ṭhākura
has made this principle clear.
Just see his profound judgement!

SECTION 19

The Lord Serves the Preachers

bhakti ahaitukī haya sva-prakāśita
nitya-siddha vastu kintu āche āvarita

bhakti – devotional service; *ahaitukī* – unmotivated; *haya* – is; *sva-prakāśita* – self-
manifest; *nitya-siddha* – eternally perfect; *vastu* – substance; *kintu* – but; *āche* – it is;
āvarita – covered.

Viśvanātha Cakravartī Ṭhākura states that the main feature of **bhakti**
is that it is causeless – it manifests only of its own accord.
Although **bhakti** is an eternally perfect substance,
it lies dormant, deep within every soul.

madhyama-adhikārī-vaiṣṇava kṛpā ta' kariyā

bāliśere kare kṛpā bhakti jāgāiyā

madhyama-adhikārī-vaiṣṇava – a middle-class devotee; *kṛpā* – mercy; *ta'* – indeed; *kariyā* – showing; *bāliśere* – to the innocent childlike non-devotees; *kare* – shows; *kṛpā* – mercy; *bhakti* – devotion; *jāgāiyā* – causes to awaken.

The middle-class devotee (*madhyama-adhikārī*)
  always extends mercy toward others.
Being compassionate to innocent, childlike souls,
  he endeavors to awaken their dormant *bhakti*.

vaiṣṇavera vaśa hana svayaṁ bhagavān
vaiṣṇavera kṛpāya mugdha haya jāguyān

vaiṣṇavera – of the devotee; *vaśa* – subservient; *hana* – is; *svayam bhagavān* – the Lord Himself; *vaiṣṇavera* – of the devotee; *kṛpāya* – by the mercy; *mugdha* – enchanted; *haya* – is; *jāguyān* – follows the leader.

The Supreme Lord Himself
  comes under the control of such a true devotee.
Being enchanted with the devotee's merciful nature,
  the Lord always follows his lead.

vaiṣṇava jāgāte pāre ghumanta jagat
tāṅ'ra-i kṛpāya haya pāpīrā bhakata

vaiṣṇava – a devotee; *jāgāte* – to awaken; *pāre* – is able to; *ghumanta* – sleeping; *jagat* – the universe; *tāṅ'ra-i* – verily his; *kṛpāya* – by the mercy; *haya* – becomes; *pāpīrā* – of sinful souls; *bhakata* – devotees.

A Vaiṣṇava is able to re-awaken
  the sleeping material universe.
Indeed, by his magnanimous mercy,
  sinful souls are transformed into devotees.

SECTION 20

Neophytes Cannot Enlighten Others

ataeva tāṅ'ra nahe "nirjana-bhajana"
kaniṣṭha-adhikāra ei – jagat-vañcana

ataeva – therefore; *tāṅ'ra* – his; *nahe* – is not; *nirjana-bhajana* – solitary worship; *kaniṣṭha*-adhikāra – those of neophyte qualification; *ei* – this; *jagat-vañcana* – cheating the world.

Therefore the true devotee never abandons preaching work
to engage in solitary worship.
Such behavior of a neophyte devotee
will cheat the entire world.

baḍa baḍa nāma-jāḍā vaiṣṇava sajjāya
pādrī sāheba āsi' mile saba tāya

baḍa baḍa – big, big; *nāma-jāḍā* – famous; *vaiṣṇava* – certain devotees; *sajjāya* – in the assembly; *pādrī sāheba* – the British Christian father; *āsi'* – arriving; *mile* – meeting; *saba* – all; *tāya* – there.

Once I observed a group of supposedly famous Vaiṣṇavas
who held big, big devotional titles.
A British Christian missionary came to Vṛndāvana
and met with them at their assembly.

puchila śrī-kṛṣṇa-līlā vṛndāvana-mājha
nā bujhāla tā're tattva vaiṣṇava-samāja

puchila – he asked; *śrī-kṛṣṇa-līlā* – about Śrī Kṛṣṇa's pastimes; *vṛndāvana-mājha* – in Vṛndāvana; *nā* – could not; *bujhāla* – inform; *tā're* – to him; *tattva* – the truth; *vaiṣṇava-samāja* – the assembly of devotees.

The priest asked those persons to explain
the pastimes that Śrī Kṛṣṇa performed in Vṛndāvana.
But in that entire gathering of so-called famous devotees,
no one could expain to him the truth of the Lord's pastimes.

kaniṣṭha-adhikārī saba śāstra nāhi bujhe
nirjane bharame śudhu ruṭi-cānā khuñje

kaniṣṭha-adhikārī – neophyte devotees; *saba* – all of them; *śāstra* – the scriptures; *nāhi* – do not; *bujhe* – understand; *nirjane* – in solitude; *bharame* – by the burden; *śudhu* – simply; *ruṭi-cānā* – chapātīs and chick peas [daily food]; *khuñje* – search.

All those big, big devotees were actually just neophytes,
who had no proper understanding of the scriptures.
Engaging in their troublesome and pretentious solitary worship,
they are simply concerned about their next meal.

SECTION 21

The Topmost Devotee is Glorious

gurudeva balechila – kaniṣṭha e' saba
eta-dine bujhilāma tāṅra vāṇī-rava

gurudeva – my spiritual master; *balechila* – had spoken; *kaniṣṭha* – neophytes; *e' saba* – all of these; *eta-dine* – today; *bujhilāma* – I have understood; *tāṅra* – his; *vāṇī-rava* – resounding statement.

My Gurudeva boldly declared,
"All these *bābājīs* in Vraja are neophytes."
Today I have finally understood
the resounding truth of what he said.

"śāstra-yukte sunipuṇa dṛḍha-śraddhā yā'ra
uttama-adhikārī sei tāraye saṁsāra"

śāstra-yukte – in scriptural conclusions; *su-nipuṇa* – very expert; *dṛḍha-śraddhā* – firm faith in Kṛṣṇa; *yā'ra* – whose; *uttama-adhikārī* – the topmost devotee; *sei* – he; *tāraye saṁsāra* – can deliver the whole world.

"One who is expert in the conclusions of the revealed scriptures
and who has firm faith in Lord Kṛṣṇa
is classified as a topmost devotee (***uttama-adhikārī***).
He can deliver the whole world." [Cc. *Madhya* 22.65]

patita-pāvana tini jagatete khyāti
e' patite uddhāraha tabe ta sukhyāti

patita-pāvana – savior of the fallen; *tini* – he; *jagatete* – throughout the universe; *khyāti* – is famous; *e'* – this; *patite* – fallen soul; *uddhāraha* – delivering; *tabe* – then; *ta* – indeed; *su-khyāti* – enhanced reputation.

My spiritual master is famous throughout the universe
as the savior of the fallen.
His fame will surely increase
if he can deliver someone as fallen as me.

kali-kālera jīva saba patita adhama
dekhiyā-o nāhi dekhe ihā ki karama

kali-kālera – in the Age of Kali; *jīva* – the souls; *saba* – all; *patita* – fallen; *adhama* – despicable; *dekhiyā-o* – although looking; *nāhi dekhe* – they can't see; *ihā* – here; *ki* – what; *karama* – the situation.

In this degraded Age of Kali-yuga,
all the souls are fallen and wretched.
Although looking with their eyes, they cannot see
the actual situation of anything in this illusory world.

SECTION 22

Devotees do not Imitate the Lord

mahā-vadānya īśvara – śrī-gaura-sundara
tāṅhāra amṛta-vāṇī madhura mukhara

mahā-vadānya – most magnanimous; *īśvara* – the Lord; *śrī-gaura-sundara* – Śrī Gaura-sundara; *tāṅhāra* – His; *amṛta-vāṇī* – nectarean words; *madhura* – sweet; *mukhara* – resounding.

Śrī Gaura-sundara, the beautiful Supreme Personality of Godhead,
is the most magnanimous personality.
His nectarean instructions to us
are sweet and profound to hear.

bhārata bhūmite janma haila yāṅhāra
tāṅhāra vāṇīte kara paropakāra

bhārata bhūmite – in the land of India; *janma haila* – having taken birth; *yāṅhāra* – whose; *tāṅhāra* – his; *vāṇīte* – on the instruction; *kara* – please do; *para-upakāra* – welfare unto others.

His instruction was that
whoever has taken birth
in the holy land of India,
should please work for the benefit of others.

nirjane āsvādana se ta' prabhura līlā
līlā anukaraṇa nahe vaiṣṇavera khelā

nirjane – in solitude; *āsvādana* – tasting; *se* – that; *ta'* – indeed; *prabhura līlā* – pastimes of the Lord; *līlā* – His pastimes; *anukaraṇa* – imitating; *nahe* – is not; *vaiṣṇavera* – of a devotee; *khelā* – the sport.

One of the Lord's own pastimes was to remain in solitude,
tasting and relishing transcendental topics.
But it is never the devotee's practice
to imitate the Lord's confidential pastimes.

sevā-kārya vaiṣṇavera nahe āsvādana
jaḍa-dehe āsvādana nahe sambhāvana

sevā-kārya – activities of service; *vaiṣṇavera* – of the devotee; *nahe* – does not; *āsvādana* – tasting; *jaḍa-dehe* – in the dull material body; *āsvādana* – tasting; *nahe* – there is not; *sambhāvana* – possibility.

**When the devotees engage in the activities of devotional service,
they never attempt to personally relish nectar as the Lord did.
Tasting and relishing transcendental pastimes is actually impossible
for those covered by a dull material body.**

SECTION 23

Caste Consciousness Condemned

dehātma-buddhi yāra sei jaḍa deha
sei dehe āsvādana nāhi kare keha

deha-ātma-buddhi – considering the body to be the self; *yāra* – whose; *sei* – he; *jaḍa deha* – material body; *sei dehe* – with that body; *āsvādana* – tasting; *nāhi kare* – does not do; *keha* – anyone.

**One who is deluded by gross bodily consciousness
identifies with the material body.
While trapped in this temporary covering, no one
can ever relish transcendental enjoyment, as the Lord did.**

vaiṣṇavete jāti-buddhi prabala pracura
līlā-āsvādane kintu baḍa bāhādura

vaiṣṇavete – unto the devotees; *jāti-buddhi* – consideration of caste; *prabala* – bold; *pracura* – very much; *līlā-āsvādane* – in tasting divine pastimes; *kintu* – but; *baḍa* – very; *bāhādura* – skillful.

There are some persons who shamelessly judge the Lord's devotees
in terms of their caste or external bodily nature,
but these same critics consider themselves quite expert
in relishing transcendental pastimes.

ḍāka-gharera kerāṇī (eka) gosāi ṭhākura
bābājī praṇāma kare tāhāre pracura

ḍāka-gharera – of the post office; *kerāṇī* – office clerk; *eka* – one; *gosāi* – a caste *gosvāmī*;
ṭhākura – a revered soul; *bābājī* – renunciants; *praṇāma kare* – bowing down; *tāhāre* –
unto him; *pracura* – very much.

For example, there is a clerk at the post office
who is a revered caste *gosvāmī*.
The local *bābājīs* always go there
and offer him respects again and again.

gosāi ṭhākura kare jāti-abhimāna
nityānanda prabhu-vare kare khāna khāna

gosāi ṭhākura – that revered soul; *kare* – maintains; *jāti-abhimāna* – pride in one's own
caste, *nityānanda* – Lord Nityānanda; *prabhu vare* – the best of Lords; *kare* – does; *khāna
khāna* – breaking into pieces.

But even that supposedly exalted *gosvāmī*
is puffed up about his own caste by birth.
Śrī Nityānanda Prabhu, the best of Lords,
smashes these misconceptions to pieces.

SECTION 24

Revival Needed in Vṛndāvana

ei kārya dekhitechi vṛndāvana-mājha
ataeva bujhi hethā āche kichu kāja

ei kārya – these activities; *dekhitechi* – I have seen; *vṛndāvana-mājha* – in Vṛndāvana; *ataeva* – therefore; *bujhi* – I understand; *hethā* – here; *āche* – there is; *kichu* – some; *kāja* – work.

> I have personally seen these things going on
> in the holy land of Vṛndāvana-dhāma.
> Therefore I can understand
> there is some work to be done here.

prākṛta-sahajiyā saba vyabhicāra kare
para-strī la'ye līlā āsvādana kare

prākṛta-sahajiyā – mundane imitators; *saba* – all; *vyabhicāra* – debauchery; *kare* – doing; *para-strī* – others' wives; *la'ye* – seducing; *līlā* – so-called pastimes; *āsvādana* – tasting; *kare* – doing.

> There are many pretentious *prākṛta-sahajiyās*
> busily engaged in outright debauchery.
> They seduce others' wives and try to relish
> a mundane imitation of transcendental *līlā*.

e nahe vṛndāvana-vāsa bhāva sadā mana
gosvāmīra pāda-padma karaha smaraṇa

e – this; *nahe* – is not; *vṛndāvana-vāsa* – residence in Vṛndāvana; *bhāva* – the ecstatic mood; *sadā* – always; *mana* – O mind; *gosvāmīra* – of the six Gosvāmīs; *pāda-padma* – the lotus feet; *karaha* – please do; *smaraṇa* – remembrance.

> These are not the ecstatic devotional moods
> of the transcendental abode of Vṛndāvana-dhāma.
> O my dear mind! Please continually remember
> the lotus feet of the six Gosvāmīs.

chaya gosāi āsi' yathā dharma pracārila
mahāprabhu-ājñāya saba bhakti vistārila

chaya gosāi – the six Gosvāmīs; *āsi'* – arriving; *yathā* – just as; *dharma* – religious principles; *pracārila* – had preached; *mahāprabhu-ājñāya* – on the order of Lord Caitanya; *saba* – all; *bhakti* – devotion; *vistārila* – had spread.

Since the time when the six Gosvāmīs arrived in Vṛndāvana
on the order of Śrī Caitanya Mahāprabhu
and preached true religious principles,
the practice of devotional service has indeed flourished everywhere.

SECTION 25

Don't Imitate, Just Preach

nitya-siddha pārṣada saba rādhā-kṛṣṇa smare
tāṅ'dera smaraṇa jīvera sarva-pāpa hare

nitya-siddha – eternally liberated; *pārṣada* – personal associates; *saba* – all of them; *rādhā-kṛṣṇa* – of Rādhā and Kṛṣṇa; *smare* – remember; *tāṅ'dera* – their; *smaraṇa* – remembrance; *jīvera* – the fallen souls; *sarva* – all; *pāpa* – sins; *hare* – are vanquished.

The six Gosvamīs are the Lord's eternally liberated associates,
and they continuously remember the pastimes of Rādhā and Kṛṣṇa.
Their confidential practice of such remembrance (*līlā-smaraṇa*)
vanquishes all the sins of fallen souls.

anukaraṇa kari' yadi sei-bhāva dhare
māyā-kavalita haya saṁsāra nā tare

anukaraṇa – imitation; *kari'* – doing; *yadi* – if; *sei* – that; *bhāva* – mood; *dhare* – accepts; *māyā-kavalita* – seized by illusion; *haya* – becomes; *saṁsāra* – from the material world; *nā* – is not; *tare* – delivered.

If someone simply imitates the Gosvamīs
  by artificially adopting their dress and behavior,
then he is immediately captured by *māyā*
  and is never allowed to escape from the material world.

pracāra karaha sadā jīva-ghare ghare
saphala haibe jīvana pracārera dvāre

pracāra – preaching; *karaha* – please do; *sadā* – always; *jīva* – fallen souls; *ghare ghare* – from home to home; *saphala* – successful; *haibe* – it will be; *jīvana* – life; *pracārera dvāre* – by means of preaching.

Just preach the Lord's message to the fallen souls,
  continually going from door to door.
By the grace of that preaching,
  your life will become truly successful.

"śrī-dayita dāsa"-prabhu dena ei śikṣā
"kara ucchaiḥ-svare nāma" ei tāṅ'ra dīkṣā

śrī-dayita dāsa – Śrī Vārṣabhānavī-Dayita dāsa [Bhaktisiddhānta Sarasvatī Prabhupāda]; *prabhu* – my master; *dena* – has given; *ei* – this; *śikṣā* – instruction; *kara* – please do; *ucchaiḥ-svare* – in a loud voice; *nāma* – the holy name; *ei* – this; *tāṅ'ra* – his; *dīkṣā* – injunction.

My spiritual master, Śrī Vārṣabhānavī-Dayita Dāsa,
  has given the following instruction:
"Chant the holy name in a loud voice!" ["*Duṣṭa Mana*" 19]
  This is his foremost commandment.

SECTION 26

Pure *Kīrtana* Replaces Radios and Newspapers

> *kīrtanera aṅga śudhu nahe ḍhāka-ḍhola*
> *ādhunika dhārāya nahe kīrtanera rola*

kīrtanera – of congregational chanting; *aṅga* – aspect; *śudhu* – only; *nahe* – not; *ḍhāka-ḍhola* – beating on drums; *ādhunika* – modern; *dhārāya* – by the style; *nahe* – not; *kīrtanera* – of congregational chanting; *rola* – the sound.

However, this performance of congregational chanting is not limited
     only to the traditional form that is accompanied by beating on drums.
All modern communication systems can be used,
     even if they do not currently transmit the sweet sound of pure *kīrtana*.

> *hari-sevāra anukūla sakala-i mādhava*
> *tri-jagatera bhoktā haya ekalā yādava*

hari-sevāra – for service to Lord Hari; *anukūla* – favorable; *sakala-i* – truly everything; *mādhava* – is actually Lord Mādhava; *tri-jagatera* – of the three worlds; *bhoktā* – the enjoyer; *haya* – is; *ekalā* – only; *yādava* – Lord of the Yadu dynasty.

All things truly useful for the service of Hari
     are spiritually nondifferent from Lord Madhava,
for in actuality the sole enjoyer of everything
     in the three worlds is Lord Yādava.

> *māyāra vaibhava yata "reḍiora" śabda*
> *kīrtanera dvārā sadā kara tāhā stabdha*

māyāra – of illusion; *vaibhava* – opulence; *yata* – all; *reḍiora* – of the radios; *śabda* – the sound; *kīrtanera dvārā* – by congregational chanting; *sadā* – always; *kara* – please do; *tāhā* – that; *stabdha* – stopped.

Māyā's deluding potency is perfectly expressed
     in the blaring mundane noise of the radios we hear everywhere.

Just put an end to all this nonsense by replacing it
with continual broadcasts of transcendental *kīrtana*.

māyāra kac-kaci saba saṁvādera patra
kīrtana karaha tāhe jagate sarvatra

māyāra – of illusion; *kac-kaci* – incessant intolerable prattling; *saba* – all; *saṁvādera* –
of news; *patra* – missive; *kīrtana* – congregational chanting; *karaha* – please do; *tāhe* – in
that; *jagate* – in the universe; *sarvatra* – everywhere.

All the mundane newspapers endlessly carry
trivial, intolerable chattering about *māyā's* endless distractions.
Just counteract all this by publishing the Lord's glories
and distributing these newspapers everywhere in the world.

SECTION 27

Loud *Kīrtana* Causes Real Advancement

ghare vase' ceṅcāiyā pitta-vṛddhi kari'
koṭi janme-o santuṣṭa habe nā śrī-hari

ghare – in the room; *vase'* – sitting; *ceṅcāiyā* – loudly vocalizing; *pitta-vṛddhi* – increase
of bile secretion [the passionate result of *pitta-doṣa* imbalance]; *kari'* – doing; *koṭi* – tens
of millions; *janme-o* – in births also; *santuṣṭa* – satisfied; *habe* – will be; *nā* – not; *śrī-*
hari – Lord Hari.

By sitting in a solitary room, pretentiously calling out to the Lord,
you may increase your bile secretion,
but by spending even ten million births in that way
you never will actually please Śrī Hari.

śrī-hari nahe kāro bābāra sampatti
"khoṅyāḍera" bāhira hao nā kara āpatti

śrī-hari – Lord Hari; *nahe* – is not; *kāro* – someone's; *bābāra* – of the renunciants; *sampatti* – sole property; *khoṅyāḍera* – of the pen; *bāhira* – outside; *hao* – may it be; *nā* – do not; *kara* – make; *āpatti* – objection.

> **Śrī Hari cannot be claimed by some *bābājīs***
> > **as their exclusive property.**
> **Just come out of your tiny little cage**
> > **and stop raising so many objections.**

> *saba śrī-harira, āra śrī-hari sabāra*
> *kara ucca-svare kīrtana – ei' śikṣā tāṅra*

saba – everyone; *śrī-harira* – is Lord Hari's; *āra* – and; *śrī-hari* – Lord Hari; *sabāra* – is everyone's; *kara* – please do; *ucca-svare* – in a loud voice; *kīrtana* – congregational chanting; *ei'* – this; *śikṣā* – instruction; *tāṅra* – his.

> **Everyone belongs to Śrī Hari,**
> > **and Śrī Hari belongs to everyone.**
> **"Go on chanting *kīrtana* with loudly raised voices!"**
> > **This is the Lord's personal instruction to all of us.**

> *kīrtana-prabhāve ha'be smaraṇa āpani*
> *nirjana-bhajana sei hṛdaye takhani*

kīrtana-prabhāve – by the influence of chanting; *ha'be* – it will be; *smaraṇa* – visualization of the Lord's daily *aṣṭa-kālīyā-līlā*; *āpani* – automatically; *nirjana-bhajana* – solitary worship; *sei* – that; *hṛdaye* – in the heart; *takhani* – forthwith.

> **By the potency of that *kīrtana*,**
> > **the process of *līlā-smaraṇa*,**
> > **remembrance of the Lord's daily pastimes,**
> > **will spontaneously arise.**
> **Only then the qualification**
> > **for solitary worship within the heart**
> > **will be genuinely attained.**

> —**Śrī Abhaya Caraṇa Bhaktivedānta**
> **Editor, *Back to Godhead***

Viraha-Aṣṭāṣṭaka

Viraha-Aṣṭāṣṭaka

"Eight Octets in Separation from My Spiritual Master" composed in 1958 by His Divine Grace A. C. Bhaktivedanta Swami Prabhupāda

INTRODUCTION

Prior to the disappearance anniversary of Śrīla Bhaktisiddhānta Sarasvatī in February of 1959, Abhay Charanaravinda Bhaktivedanta keenly felt separation from his spiritual master. He understood that Śrīla Bhaktisiddhānta's instructions were more important than his physical presence and that, in fact, the spiritual master is present within his instructions. In this way Abhay had always been with him. Yet on this particular annual observance, Abhay keenly felt his exceptional loss. He remembered how in 1932 he had been a *gṛhastha* and a new disciple. He had not been free then to do as much service as he was doing now. Yet it had been in those years that he personally saw his spiritual master, offered obeisances before him, ate the remnants of his *prasādam*, walked beside him, heard his voice, and received his glance. Abhay thought deeply of their meetings together.

How powerful had been Śrīla Bhaktisiddhānta's mission! His presses had been running day and night, printing magazines, books, the daily *Nadīyā Prakāśa* newspaper. And Europe had been a promising new preaching field. With Śrīla Bhaktisiddhānta Sarasvatī Ṭhākura at the helm, the Gauḍīya Maṭha had entered into battle against *māyā's* forces, and Śrīla Bhaktisiddhānta had made his disciples fearless.

Abhay had always been eager to serve his spiritual master, to cooperate with the Gauḍīya Maṭha, and with its headquarters in Calcutta. But exactly how he would serve had not been clear to him until he received his last letter from Śrīla Bhaktisiddhānta Sarasvatī, wherein he was urged to continue preaching the message of Śrīman Mahāprabhu to the English-speaking world.

Abhay looked back on the more than twenty years since his spiritual master's disappearance. The Gauḍīya Maṭha had been undone by its leaders, and everyone else had scattered like leaves in a storm. It was an unspeakable loss. And it was an old story – how the big *sannyāsīs* had disregarded their spiritual master's instructions and instead created intrigues, disputes, litigations, violent party factions, false leaders claiming to be world *ācārya* – and which party had been right? No, both had been wrong, all wrong, because the Gauḍīya Maṭha had disintegrated. Now there were dozens of little *mathas* and no preaching, no real preaching as before, when he, Siṁha-guru, had cast fear into the hearts of the Māyāvādīs, and had led an army of young powerful preachers to march throughout India and the world. And the greatest casualties of the Gauḍīya Maṭha's dissolution were the people, the nondevotees, who now had little hope of being delivered from *māyā's* batterings. Śrīla Bhaktisiddhānta Sarasvatī had begun a spiritual revolution, but now *māyā* had overthrown that revolution. The scattered remnants of the Gauḍīya Maṭha had settled quietly into self-satisfied, insular, almost impotent units. And it was the people in general who suffered the tragic loss of the *saṅkīrtana* movement.

Abhay clung to memories of his *guru*. He felt secure, in that his own relationship with Śrīla Bhaktisiddhānta Sarasvatī was intact and ongoing. Yet he felt some helplessness. He was diligently pursuing his spiritual master's order to preach in English, but without his spiritual master's physical presence he felt inadequate and alone. At times like this, he questioned the wisdom of having left his family and business.

Lamenting Śrīla Bhaktisiddhānta's absence and the fall of the Gauḍīya Maṭha, he composed a Bengali poem in December 1958 named *Viraha-Aṣṭāṣṭaka* ("Eight Octets in Separation from My Spiritual Master"). Abhay's was a dark view at this time. The golden era of preaching that had flourished in Śrīla Bhaktisiddhānta Sarasvatī's day was no longer. "Now, by the influence of *māyā*," Abhay wrote, "there is only darkness everywhere."

Meditating on that great personality possessed of the divine power to save the world, Abhay expressed his feelings of weakness and helplessness. Now who could save the entire world, which was more oppressed than before? Śrīla Bhaktisiddhānta had said that a dead man cannot preach; only one with life could preach. Abhay realized that as long as he and others could deeply regret the Gauḍīya Maṭha's failure, there was still life and still hope. It was useless to cry over what his godbrothers had done, yet in seeing and resenting it, Abhay found, within the pain of what might have been, an abiding spark of what still might be: His spiritual master had instructed everyone to chant, and "You empowered everyone with the further qualification **to** distribute that holy name."

Abhay Charanaravinda Bhaktivedanta sent this poem to his godbrother Keśava Mahārāja, who published it in the *Gauḍīya Patrikā* magazine under the title "Eight Stanzas on Separation from Bhaktisiddhānta Sarasvatī" in Volume X, Number 11 (February 1959), in time for Śrīla Bhaktisiddhānta Sarasvatī's disappearance anniversary.

Octet headings

1 ~ The Flood of *Kṛṣṇa-prema*

2 ~ The Merciful Flood has been Stopped

3 ~ Practical Chanting and Preaching

4 ~ The Essential Purport Neglected

5 ~ The Disciple's Empowerment is Lost

6 ~ The Preaching Mission is Scattered

7 ~ The Pure Devotional Process

8 ~ If Only You Would Come Again

Viraha-Aṣṭāṣṭaka

"Eight Octets in Separation from My Spiritual Master"

Prathama Aṣṭaka
First Octet

The Flood of *Kṛṣṇa-prema*

(1) *jīvera darada-duḥkhī śrīla prabhupāda!*
viraha-vāsare tava heri avasāda

jīvera – of the conditioned souls; *darada* – pain; *duḥkhī* – he who suffers; *śrīla prabhupāda* – O Śrīla Bhaktisiddhānta Sarasvatī Prabhupāda; *viraha-vāsare* – on the anniversary of the day of separation; *tava* – your; *heri* – I behold; *avasāda* – loss of spirit.

O Śrīla Prabhupāda! You personally suffer
to see the suffering of the fallen conditioned souls.
On this anniversary of your separation
I feel utterly despondent.

(2) *ābaddha-karuṇā-sindhu kāṭiyā mohāna*
nityānanda karechila prema-vanyā dāna

ābaddha – sealed; *karuṇā-sindhu* – the ocean of mercy; *kāṭiyā* – cutting; *mohāna* – a channel; *nityānanda* – Lord Nityānanda; *karechila* – had done; *prema-vanyā* – flood of divine love; *dāna* – the gift.

"The ocean of mercy was previously dammed up,
but Lord Nityānanda Himself cut open a channel,
thereby releasing an outpouring flood
of pure ecstatic love of God."
[from Locana Dāsa Ṭhākura's "*Nitai guṇa-maṇi*"]

(3) *yādera kavale chila srota pravāhite*
tādera bādhila māyā vrata para-hite

yādera – of whom; *kavale* – in the grip; *chila* – had been; *srota* – the current; *pravāhite* – in the flowing; *tādera* – their; *bādhila* – obstructed; *māyā* – illusory energy; *vrata* – ceremonies; *para-hite* – for the benefit of others.

> Those devotees to whom the responsibility was given
> to continue spreading this flood of love
> somehow became overpowered by *māyā*
> and were reduced to simply performing
> ritualistic Hindu ceremonies for the benefit of materialists.

(4)   *jāti-gosāi nāme tā'rā pravāha bādhila*
        āpani āsiyā prabhu muhānā khulila

jāti-gosāi – the caste *gosvāmīs*; *nāme* – by name; *tā'rā* – their; *pravāha* – the flow; *bādhila* – blocked; *āpani* – personally; *āsiyā* – coming; *prabhu* – O master; *muhānā* – the channel; *khulila* – have opened.

> Lord Nityānanda's inundation of *prema* was thus obstructed
> by those known as *jātī-gosāi*, or caste *gosvāmīs*.
> But then you personally came, O Master,
> to open wide the floodgates once again.

(5)   *premera vanyāya ābāra ḍubāla sabāre*
        mo-hena dīna hīna patita pāmare

premera – of divine love; *vanyāya* – in the flood; *ābāra* – again; *ḍubāla* – caused to immerse; *sabāre* – to everyone; *mo-hena* – such as me; *dīna hīna* – humble and destitute; *patita pāmare* – to the fallen, sinful one.

> Again you engulfed everyone
> in the deluge of pure divine love –
> even such a low, wretched, fallen,
> and sinful soul as me.

(6)   *mahāprabhura ājñā-bale sevaka sabāre*
        guru-rūpe pāṭhāle jīvera dvāre dvāre

mahāprabhura – of Lord Caitanya; *ājñā-bale* – on the strength of the command; *sevaka* – servants; *sabāre* – to all; *guru-rūpe* – in the form of spiritual masters; *pāṭhāle* – had sent; *jīvera* – of the fallen souls; *dvāre dvāre* – from door to door.

> On the strength of Lord Caitanya Mahāprabhu's command,
> you sent out all your servants
> as spiritual masters, from door to door,
> just to deliver the fallen souls.

(7) *ā-samudra himācala sarvatra pracāra*
tomāra virahe āja saba andhakāra

ā-samudra – extending from the ocean; *himācala* – to the Himālaya mountains; *sarvatra* – everywhere; *pracāra* – preaching; *tomāra* – your; *virahe* – in separation; *āja* – today; *saba* – everything; *andhakāra* – is darkness.

> The devotees were preaching everywhere,
> from the oceans to the Himālayas.
> But now that you are gone from our midst,
> there is only darkness everywhere.

(8) *jīvera darada-duḥkhī śrīla prabhupāda!*
viraha-vāsare tava heri avasāda

jīvera – of the conditioned souls; *darada* – pain; *duḥkhī* – he who suffers; *śrīla prabhupāda* – O Śrīla Bhaktisiddhānta Sarasvatī Prabhupāda; *viraha-vāsare* – on the anniversary of the day of separation; *tava* – your; *heri* – I behold; *avasāda* – loss of spirit.

> O Śrīla Prabhupāda! You personally suffer
> to see the suffering of the fallen conditioned souls.
> On this day of your separation
> I am utterly despondent.

Dvitīya Aṣṭaka
Second Octet

The Merciful Flood has been Stopped

(1)   *advaita prabhu yemana gaura enechila*
       bhaktivinoda prabhu tathā nivedila

advaita – Advaita; *prabhu* – the master; *yemana* – just as; *gaura* – Lord Caitanya; *enechila* – had brought; *bhaktivinoda* – Bhaktivinoda Ṭhākura; *prabhu* – the master; *tathā* – like that; *nivedila* – had prayed.

Just as Advaita Prabhu fervently prayed
    and thus induced Śrī Gaurāṅga to descend,
your father, Bhaktivinoda Ṭhākura,
    prayed for you to incarnate.

(2)   *tāṅhāra-i āgrahe prabhu! esechile tumi*
       bujhāle sakale tumi, bhārata – puṇya bhūmi

tāṅhāra-i – verily his; *āgrahe* – by zeal; *prabhu* – O master; *esechile* – have come; *tumi* – you; *bujhāle* – have informed; *sakale* – everyone; *tumi* – you; *bhārata* – India; *puṇya bhūmi* – holy land.

Because of Śrīla Bhaktivinoda's ardent desire, O Master,
    you came and proclaimed to everyone
that India is the holy land
    of the Lord's divine pastimes.

(3)   *"bhārata-bhūmite janma haila yāhāra*
       janma sārthaka kari' kara paropakāra"

bhārata-bhūmite – in the land of India; *janma* – birth; *haila* – has accepted; *yāhāra* – of whom; *janma* – such a birth; *sārthaka* – perfection; *kari'* – doing so; *kara* – please do; *para* – unto others; *upakāra* – welfare work.

"One who has taken his birth as a human being
    in the land of India

should make his life successful and work
for the benefit of all other people." [Cc. Ādi 9.41]

(4) *ei mahā-mantra vāṇī sarvatra pracāra*
tomāra virahe prabhu! saba andhakāra

ei – this; *mahā-mantra* – great message; *vāṇī* – the words; *sarvatra* – everywhere; *pracāra* – preaching; *tomāra* – your; *virahe* – in separation; *prabhu* – O master; *saba* – everything; *andhakāra* – is darkness.

Everywhere you went, you boldly preached
this great message of Lord Caitanya.
But now in your absence, O Master,
everything has fallen into darkness.

(5) *tomāra karuṇā-sindhu punaḥ baddha ha'la*
e-śela baḍa-i duḥkha bukete bājila

tomāra – your; *karuṇā-sindhu* – ocean of mercy; *punaḥ* – again; *baddha* – closed up; *ha'la* – has become; *e-śela* – this spear; *baḍa-i* – very much; *duḥkha* – unhappiness; *bukete* – in the heart; *bājila* – has struck.

The overflowing ocean of your compassion
has once again become dammed up.
Seeing this, my heart has been pierced
by the sharp spear of grief.

(6) *mahāprabhura kathā vinā saba kolāhala*
dekhiyā vaiṣṇava-kula viraha-vihvala

mahāprabhura – of Lord Caitanya; *kathā* – the message; *vinā* – without; *saba* – everything; *kolāhala* – confusion; *dekhiyā* – beholding; *vaiṣṇava-kula* – the assembly of devotees; *viraha-vihvala* – bewildered in separation.

Without Caitanya Mahāprabhu's message being spread,
there is confusion and upheaval everywhere.
Seeing this, all Vaiṣṇavas feel overwhelmed
in the pangs of your separation.

(7)   *māyā-baddha jīva-kula punaḥ andhakāre*
          śānti khuṅji mare saba ākula pāthāre

māyā-baddha – bound by illusion; *jīva-kula* – the assembly of spirit souls; *punaḥ* – again; *andhakāre* – in darkness; *śānti* – peace; *khuṅji* – searching; *mare* – are dying; *saba* – everyone; *ākula* – extremely worried; *pāthāre* – in the ocean.

> The spirit souls have once again been captured by *māyā*
> and covered by the darkness of ignorance.
> Desperately seeking relief, they are simply perishing
> in a fathomless ocean of anxiety.

(8)   *jīvera darada-duḥkhī śrīla prabhupāda!*
          viraha-vāsare tava heri avasāda

jīvera – of the conditioned souls; *darada* – pain; *duḥkhī* – he who suffers; *śrīla prabhupāda* – O Śrīla Bhaktisiddhānta Sarasvatī Prabhupāda; *viraha-vāsare* – on the anniversary of the day of separation; *tava* – your; *heri* – I behold; *avasāda* – loss of spirit.

> O Śrīla Prabhupāda! You personally suffer
> to see the suffering of the fallen conditioned souls.
> On this day of your separation
> I am utterly despondent.

Tṛtīya Aṣṭaka
Third Octet

Practical Chanting and Preaching

(1) *kṛṣṇa-nāma upadeśi tāra' sarva-jana*
sei mantra dile tumi karṇe anukṣaṇa

kṛṣṇa-nāma – the holy name of Kṛṣṇa; *upadeśi* – the instructor; *tāra'* – their; *sarva-jana* – all people; *sei* – that; *mantra* – sound formula; *dile* – gave; *tumi* – you; *karṇe* – in the ear; *anukṣaṇa* – incessantly.

You instructed everyone you met
to chant Lord Kṛṣṇa's holy name.
You showed the example by continually reciting
the *mahā-mantra* into everyone's ears.

(2) *mantra pracārite dile sabe adhikāra*
māyāra prabhāve āji saba andhakāra

mantra – the sound formula; *pracārite* – to preach; *dile* – gave; *sabe* – to all; *adhikāra* – the qualification; *māyāra* – of illusion; *prabhāve* – by the potency; *āji* – today; *saba* – everything; *andhakāra* – is darkness.

You empowered everyone with the further qualification
to distribute that holy name.
But now, by the influence of *māyā*,
there is only darkness everywhere.

(3) *bhajana-parāyaṇa jīva nṛtya-gīta kare*
guru-pada anusari jagat nistāre

bhajana-parāyaṇa – fond of performing worship; *jīva* – spirit souls; *nṛtya-gīta* – dancing and singing; *kare* – doing; *guru-pada* – the feet of the spiritual master; *anusari* – following; *jagat* – the universe; *nistāre* – saving.

The souls truly attached to worshiping the Lord
always sing and dance in joyful *saṅkīrtana*.

Following in the footsteps of their spiritual master,
    they deliver the whole world.

(4)   *anadhikārī jana kare nirjana-bhajana*
      svecchācārī kare saba indriya-tarpaṇa

anadhikārī – unqualified; *jana* – persons; *kare* – perform; *nirjana-bhajana* – solitary worship; *svecchā-ācārī* – acting on their own accord; *kare* – doing; *saba* – all; *indriya-tarpaṇa* – gratifying the senses.

But those with no such qualification perform **nirjana bhajana**,
    so-called confidential worship in a solitary place.
Thus acting whimsically, all of them actually remain absorbed
    in personal sense gratification.

(5)   *"naitat samācarej jātu manasāpi hy anīśvaraḥ"*
      bhakti-upadeśa saba haila naśvara

na – not; *etat* – this; *samācaret* – should perform; *jātu* – ever; *manasā api* – even in the mind; *hi* – certainly; *anīśvaraḥ* – one who is not a controller; *bhakti-upadeśa* – instructions on devotion; *saba* – all; *haila* – has become; *naśvara* – destroyed.

[As stated in the *Śrīmad-Bhāgavatam* (10.33.30)]:
"An ordinary soul should never imitate the activities
    of the Supreme Lord, even in his mind."
For those indulging in such imitation,
    the teachings of pure devotional service are all spoiled.

(6)   *āsakti-rahita yogya-viṣaya-vyavahāra*
      sahaja upāya-siddhi tomāra pracāra

āsakti-rahita – without attachment; *yogya-viṣaya* – appropriate objects; *vyavahāra* – behavior; *sahaja* – easy; *upāya-siddhi* – perfect means; *tomāra* – your; *pracāra* – preaching.

You preached that utility is the principle –
    one should act with detachment
    while using appropriate things procured by modest means
      in the Lord's service.

(7) *nirbandha kṛṣṇa-sevā ghare ghare maṭha*
    viparīta sajjāya āja sarvatra prakaṭa

nirbandha – a happening; *kṛṣṇa-sevā* – service of Kṛṣṇa; *ghare ghare* – in each and every home; *maṭha* – temple; *viparīta* – opposite; *sajjāya* – in arrangement; *āja* – today; *sarvatra* – everywhere; *prakaṭa* – evident.

> **In such detached devotional service to Lord Kṛṣṇa,**
> **each and every house would become a temple.**
> **But these days, wherever one looks**
> **the exact opposite is evident.**

(8) *jīvera darada-duḥkhī śrīla prabhupāda!*
    viraha-vāsare tava heri avasāda

jīvera – of the conditioned souls; *darada* – pain; *duḥkhī* – he who suffers; *śrīla prabhupāda* – O Śrīla Bhaktisiddhānta Sarasvatī Prabhupāda; *viraha-vāsare* – on the anniversary of the day of separation; *tava* – your; *heri* – I behold; *avasāda* – loss of spirit.

> **O Śrīla Prabhupāda! You personally suffer**
> **to see the suffering of the fallen conditioned souls.**
> **On this day of your separation**
> **I am utterly despondent.**

Caturtha Aṣṭaka
Fourth Octet

The Essential Purport Neglected

(1) *ṛddhi siddhi yāhā kichu tava vākya sāra*
    "vraja-vāsīra prāṇa āche se-hetu pracāra"

ṛddhi – prosperity; *siddhi* – mystic perfection; *yāhā kichu* – whatever; *tava* – your; *vākya* – statement; *sāra* – the essence; *vraja-vāsīra* – of the residents of Vraja; *prāṇa* – life force; *āche* – there is; *se-hetu* – for that reason; *pracāra* – they preach.

Everything regarding material prosperity and mystic perfection
was fully present in your transcendental message when you said:
"Because the residents of Vraja have life,
therefore they engage in preaching work." ["*Duṣṭa Mana*" 18]

(2) *"vyavasāyātmikā buddhi" cakravartīra vicāra*
māyā-moha-pāśe āja ha'la chāra-khāra

vyavasāya-ātmikā – resolute in Kṛṣṇa consciousness; *buddhi* – the intelligence; *cakravartīra* – of Viśvanātha Cakravartī; *vicāra* – deliberation; *māyā-moha* – bewilderment by illusion; *pāśe* – in the noose; *āja* – today; *ha'la* – has become; *chāra-khāra* – ruined.

The "resolute intelligence" (*vyavasāyātmikā buddhi*)
explained by Śrīla Viśvanātha Cakravartī
[in his commentary on *Bg.* 2.41]
is now spoiled, since your disciples have become ensnared
in the bewildering noose of *māyā*.

(3) *bahu-śākhā vistārila avyavasāyī hāte*
pratiṣṭhā bāghinī āsi' yoga dila tāte

bahu-śākhā – having many branches; *vistārila* – have expanded; *avyavasāyī* – those who are irresolute; *hāte* – by manipulation; *pratiṣṭhā* – reputation; *bāghinī* – the tigress; *āsi'* – coming; *yoga* – an expedient; *dila* – given; *tāte* – on account of that.

Those who are irresolute in performing
devotional service as you instructed
have divided your mission into many factions.
The tigress of ambition for material name and fame
appeared and personally provoked this upheaval.

(4) *tomāra marama kathā nā paśila kāṇe*
yogyatā kothāya pā'ba nāma-saṅkīrtane

tomāra – your; *marama* – internal; *kathā* – message; *nā* – has not; *paśila* – entered; *kāṇe* – the ears; *yogyatā* – fitness; *kothāya* – where; *pā'ba* – will I receive; *nāma-saṅkīrtane* – for chanting the holy name.

> The essential purport of your message
> obviously did not enter their ears.
> Oh, where will I get the strength myself
> to perform this *hari-nāma-saṅkīrtana?*

(5) *nāma-gāna sei haya śrī-gurura vāṇī*
    bhuliyā-o e-kathā satya nāhi māni

nāma-gāna – singing the holy name; *sei* – that; *haya* – is; *śrī-gurura* – of the divine spiritual master; *vāṇī* – the command; *bhuliyā-o* – also neglecting; *e-kathā* – this message; *satya* – right; *nāhi* – it is not; *māni* – I consider.

> To chant the Lord's holy name is the command
> of my worshipful spiritual master.
> I do not think it is right
> to disregard that order.

(6) *tava mukhya kīrti – para-dharama vistāra*
    mahā-mantra māne yei tāra adhikāra

tava – your; *mukhya* – foremost; *kīrti* – glory; *para-dharama* – transcendent religious culture; *vistāra* – expansion; *mahā-mantra* – the holy name; *māne* – by accepting; *yei* – which; *tāra* – their; *adhikāra* – qualification.

> Your greatest distinction is that you expanded
> the topmost religious culture.
> Anyone accepting the Hare Kṛṣṇa *mahā-mantra* from you
> becomes spiritually qualified.

(7) *adhikāra lābhe yadi sabe śiṣya kare*
    tabe ta duḥkhita jīva saṁsāra nistāre

adhikāra – qualification; *lābhe* – attaining; *yadi* – if; *sabe* – they; *śiṣya kare* – make disciples; *tabe* – then; *ta* – indeed; *duḥkhita jīva* – unhappy souls; *saṁsāra* – the world; *nistāre* – rescued.

If all those who attained this qualification
were to go out and make disciples,
then the miserable conditioned souls would be delivered
from the world of birth and death.

(8) *jīvera darada-duḥkhī śrīla prabhupāda!*
viraha-vāsare tava heri avasāda

jīvera – of the conditioned souls; *darada* – pain; *duḥkhī* – he who suffers; *śrīla prabhupāda* – O Śrīla Bhaktisiddhānta Sarasvatī Prabhupāda; *viraha-vāsare* – on the anniversary of the day of separation; *tava* – your; *heri* – I behold; *avasāda* – loss of spirit.

O Śrīla Prabhupāda! You personally suffer
to see the suffering of the fallen conditioned souls.
On this day of your separation
I am utterly despondent.

Pañcama Aṣṭaka
Fifth Octet

The Disciple's Empowerment is Lost

(1)   *"hare kṛṣṇa" mahā-nāma batriśa akṣare*
        mūḍhatāya vaśībhūta kīrtana nā kare

hare kṛṣṇa – the names Hare Kṛṣṇa; *mahā-nāma* – the greatest names; *batriśa* – thirty-two; *akṣare* – syllables; *mūḍhatāya* – in foolishness; *vaśībhūta* – under the control of; *kīrtana* – chanting; *nā* – not; *kare* – doing.

The greatest *mantra* of all, consisting of thirty-two syllables, is:
Hare Kṛṣṇa Hare Kṛṣṇa, Kṛṣṇa Kṛṣṇa Hare Hare
Hare Rāma Hare Rāma, Rāma Rāma Hare Hare.
Those controlled by foolishness refuse to chant.

(2)   *tomāra upadeśa tyaji śṛgāla-vāsudevā*
        ghaṭā'la jañjāla āja sahajiyā-sevā

tomāra – your; *upadeśa* – instruction; *tyaji* – giving up; *śṛgāla* – the jackal; *vāsudevā* – Ananta Vāsudeva [the disciple of Bhaktisiddhānta Sarasvatī who tried to make himself the "successor *guru*," but later fell down]; *ghaṭā'la* – had caused; *jañjāla* – trouble; *āja* – today; *sahajiyā-sevā* – an institutional arrangement to worship supposedly advanced *gurus*, who are actually imitative *prākṛta-sahajiyās*.

Your so-called disciple, the jackal named Ananta Vāsudeva,
        disobeyed your final instruction to keep the mission united
and thereby created a scandalous fiasco,
        the result of which is evident to this day,
as imitative *prākṛta-sahajiyās* are being worshiped as *gurus* in your temples.

(3)   *kothāya rahila tomāra upadeśa-vāṇī*
        "punar-mūṣika" saba haila āpani

kothāya – where; *rahila* – has been preserved; *tomāra* – your; *upadeśa-vāṇī* – words of instruction; *punaḥ-mūṣika* – "again become a mouse" [referring to a story in the Sanskrit *Hitopadeśa*, wherein a distressed mouse approaches a sage to be transformed into a cat, a dog, and then a tiger, and is finally turned back into a mouse]; *saba* – everyone; *haila* – has become; *āpani* – personally.

> Is there a single temple to be found
>> where your instructions are still followed?
> As it is said, *punar mūṣiko bhava:*
>> Everyone has "again become a mouse."

(4) *siṁhera śāvaka āja śṛgālera chale*
   paḍiyā kāṅdiche sabe māyāra kabale

siṁhera – of a lion; *śāvaka* – the cub; *āja* – today; *śṛgālera* – of the jackal; *chale* – by the trick; *paḍiyā* – falling; *kāṅdiche* – weeping; *sabe* – everyone; *māyāra* – of illusion; *kabale* – in the grasp.

> The lion's cub has been stolen away
>> by the deceptive tricks of the jackal.
> Now everyone caught in *māyā's* mighty clutches
>> is reduced to weeping.

(5) *kṛpā yadi kara prabhu! ābāra mo'dera*
   maraṇera tīre tabe heri herapheru

kṛpā – mercy; *yadi* – if; *kara* – you show; *prabhu* – O master; *ābāra* – once more; *mo'dera* – ours; *maraṇera* – of death; *tīre* – on the shore; *tabe* – then; *heri* – I see; *heraphera* – a change.

> O Master! If you are merciful to us once again,
>> then even though we are trapped here
> on the shore of the ocean of death,
>> we will finally behold a change for the better.

(6) *tabe punaḥ sukhe morā kṛṣṇa-nāma smari*
   tomāra vaikuṇṭha-vākye dṛḍha viśvāsa kari'

tabe – then; *punaḥ* – again; *sukhe* – happily; *morā* – our; *kṛṣṇa-nāma* – the name of Kṛṣṇa; *smari* – we remember; *tomāra* – your; *vaikuṇṭha* – of the spiritual world; *vākye* – in the words; *dṛḍha* – resolute; *viśvāsa* – faith; *kari'* – we do.

Then, once again, we can blissfully meditate
on the holy name of Kṛṣṇa,
and once again have firm faith
in your Vaikuṇṭha messages.

(7)   *sei śuddha-nāma kṛṣṇa ābāra nācābe*
      māyā jañjāla saba āpani ghucibe

sei – that; *śuddha-nāma* – pure name; *kṛṣṇa* – Kṛṣṇa Himself; *ābāra* – once more; *nācābe* – will cause to dance; *māyā* – of illusion; *jañjāla* – disturbance; *saba* – all; *āpani* – by itself; *ghucibe* – will vanquish.

Once again, the pure holy name of Kṛṣṇa
will make us dance.
Thus all the confusion caused by *māyā*
will be automatically dispelled.

(8)   *jīvera darada-duḥkhī śrīla prabhupāda!*
      viraha-vāsare tava heri avasāda

jīvera – of the conditioned souls; *darada* – pain; *duḥkhī* – he who suffers; *śrīla prabhupāda* – O Śrīla Bhaktisiddhānta Sarasvatī Prabhupāda; *viraha-vāsare* – on the anniversary of the day of separation; *tava* – your; *heri* – I behold; *avasāda* – loss of spirit.

O Śrīla Prabhupāda! You personally suffer
to see the suffering of the fallen conditioned souls.
On this day of your separation
I am utterly despondent.

Ṣaṣṭha Aṣṭaka
Sixth Octet

The Preaching Mission is Scattered

(1)   *"nāca gāo bhakta-saṅge kara saṅkīrtana"*
baḍa-i madhura – mahāprabhura vacana

nāca – please dance; *gāo* – please sing; *bhakta-saṅge* – in the association of devotees; *kara* – please perform; *saṅkīrtana* – loud congregational chanting; *baḍa-i* – truly great; *madhura* – sweet; *mahāprabhura* – of Lord Caitanya; *vacana* – the statement.

"Continue dancing, singing and performing *saṅkīrtana*
in the association of devotees." [Cc. Ādi 7.92]
These words spoken by Śrī Caitanya Mahāprabhu
are especially nectarean.

(2)   *gurudeva-vākye yadi dṛḍha-śraddhā haya*
tabe saṅkīrtane kṛṣṇa-prema upajaya

gurudeva-vākye – in the words of the spiritual master; *yadi* – if; *dṛḍha-śraddhā* – firm faith; *haya* – there is; *tabe* – then; *saṅkīrtane* – in the congregational chanting; *kṛṣṇa-prema* – love for Kṛṣṇa; *upajaya* – awakens.

If we have complete faith in these instructions
given by you, our spiritual master,
then in our performance of *saṅkīrtana*
actual love for Kṛṣṇa will be aroused in us.

(3)   *prema vinā nija-buddhi saba māyā-jāla*
lābha nā haila ithe ghaṭila jañjāla

prema – love of God; *vinā* – without; *nija-buddhi* – one's own independent intelligence; *saba* – all; *māyā-jāla* – network of illusion; *lābha* – attainment; *nā* – not; *haila* – having come about; *ithe* – in this; *ghaṭila* – has become; *jañjāla* – disturbance.

Without love of God, our tiny individual intelligence
>only becomes entangled in the network of *māyā's* delusions.
Because no one actually attained *prema*,
>now there has been a great upheaval in your mission.

(4)   *māyāvādī bha're gela jagat saṁsāre*
>*vaiṣṇava chāḍila pracāra nirjanera ghare*

māyāvādī – impersonalists; *bha're* – filled; *gela* – has gone; *jagat saṁsāre* – the material world; *vaiṣṇava* – the devotees; *chāḍila* – have given up; *pracāra* – preaching; *nirjanera* – of solitary; *ghare* – in the cottage.

The whole world has become filled with impersonalists,
>and the Vaiṣṇavas have given up
the work of preaching that was entrusted to them
>and gone off to perform solitary worship.

(5)   *patita-pāvana nāme paḍila kalaṅka*
>*chāḍāchāḍi ha'la saba vaiṣṇava asaṅkhya*

patita-pāvana – deliverer of the fallen; *nāme* – by name; *paḍila* – has fallen; *kalaṅka* – scandalous; *chāḍāchāḍi* – estrangement; *ha'la* – have become; *saba* – all; *vaiṣṇava* – the devotees; *asaṅkhya* – innumerable.

The Vaiṣṇavas were famous as *patita-pāvana*, deliverers of the fallen,
>but now this title has fallen into disgrace.
Countless numbers of your disciples
>have been alienated from your movement.

(6)   *e hena durdine prabhu! ki habe upāya?*
>*tomāra sājāna bāgāna bhāṅgiyā ye yāya*

e – this; *hena* – such; *dur-dine* – on the bad day; *prabhu* – O master; *ki habe* – what will be; *upāya* – the remedy; *tomāra* – your; *sājāna* – arrayed; *bāgāna* – garden; *bhāṅgiyā* – broken and scattered; *ye* – which; *yāya* – gone.

At such an inauspicious time, O Master,
>what can be done to repair this damage?

The beautiful garden you so carefully planted
is now uprooted and scattered about.

(7) *subuddhi jāgāo prabhu! e kṣudra antare*
tomāra kathāya yāte dṛḍha-śraddhā bāḍe

su-buddhi – good intelligence; *jāgāo* – please awaken; *prabhu* – O master; *e* – this; *kṣudra* – tiny; *antare* – within; *tomāra* – your; *kathāya* – in the message; *yāte* – by which; *dṛḍha-śraddhā* – firm faith; *bāḍe* – increases.

O Master, please awaken some good intelligence
in this insignificant disciple of yours
so that my firm faith in your transcendental message
may increase more and more.

(8) *jīvera darada-duḥkhī śrīla prabhupāda!*
viraha-vāsare tava heri avasāda

jīvera – of the conditioned souls; *darada* – pain; *duḥkhī* – he who suffers; *śrīla prabhupāda* – O Śrīla Bhaktisiddhānta Sarasvatī Prabhupāda; *viraha-vāsare* – on the anniversary of the day of separation; *tava* -- your; *heri* – I behold; *avasāda* – loss of spirit.

O Śrīla Prabhupāda! You personally suffer
to see the suffering of the fallen conditioned souls.
On this day of your separation
I am utterly despondent.

Saptama Aṣṭaka
Seventh Octet

Distributing the Pure Devotional Process

(1) *mahā-vadānya avatāra śrī-kṛṣṇa-caitanya*
      kṛṣṇa-nāma-prema diyā viśva kaila dhanya

mahā-vadānya – greatly magnanimous; *avatāra* – incarnation; *śrī-kṛṣṇa-caitanya* – Lord Caitanya; *kṛṣṇa-nāma-prema* – love for the holy name of Kṛṣṇa; *diyā* – gave; *viśva* – the universe; *kaila* – had made; *dhanya* – fortunate.

The Lord's most magnanimous form was Śrī Kṛṣṇa Caitanya.
Distributing a process of attaining love of God
by chanting Kṛṣṇa's holy name,
He blessed this whole universe.

(2) *āpani sei ta' prabhu! mūrta gaura-vāṇī*
      pṛthivīra sarva-grāme sei nāma dāni

āpani – yourself; *sei* – that; *ta'* – indeed; *prabhu* – O master; *mūrta* – personification; *gaura-vāṇī* – the message of Lord Caitanya; *pṛthivīra* – of the earth; *sarva-grāme* – in all the towns; *sei* – that; *nāma* – holy name; *dāni* – the distributor.

O Master, you are the personification
of Lord Caitanya's transcendental message.
You are the distributor of that message
to every town and village of the world.

(3) *pāṭhāilā nija bhakte sudūra pāścātye*
      bhārata bhramile nije āra dākṣiṇātye

pāṭhāilā – had sent; *nija* – own; *bhakte* – devotees; *su-dūra* – very far; *pāścātye* – to the West; *bhārata* – India; *bhramile* – travelled; *nije* – personally; *āra* – also; *dākṣiṇātye* – in South India.

You sent your devotees to preach
in the faraway lands of the Western countries,

and you personally traveled all over India,
> both north and south.

(4) *śuddha gaura-gāthā yāte vijña-jana bujhe*
> *kata cintā kara prabhu! virodhīke yujhe*

śuddha – pure; *gaura-gāthā* – topics of Lord Caitanya; *yāte* – by which; *vijña-jana* – intelligent people; *bujhe* – understanding; *kata* – how much; *cintā* – concern; *kara* – you show; *prabhu* – O master; *virodhīke* – with the unfavorable persons; *yujhe* – contending with.

You preached Lord Gaurāṅga's pure philosophy
> in such a way that intelligent persons could understand.
And you showed great concern, O Master,
> in persuading all your adversaries.

(5) *jīva nistārite gaura kare ye cāturī*
> *āpani bujhile sei-saba bhāri-bhūri*

jīva – fallen souls; *nistārite* – to deliver; *gaura* – Lord Caitanya; *kare* – enacts; *ye* – which; *cāturī* – clever tricks; *āpani* – yourself; *bujhile* – understood; *sei-saba* – all those; *bhāri-bhūri* – fully.

Lord Gaurāṅga devised many clever schemes to engage
> the conditioned souls in devotional service,
and you understood how to fully use
> all those same tactics.

(6) *deśa-kāla-pātra jāni pracāra-prabandha*
> *dekhiyā-o nāhi dekhe ulūkādi andha*

deśa-kāla-pātra – place, time, and recipients; *jāni* – knowing; *pracāra* – preaching; *prabandha* – stratagem; *dekhiyā-o* – although looking; *nāhi* – not; *dekhe* – they see; *ulūka-ādi* – owls and so forth; *andha* – blind.

You understood time, place, and circumstance,
> and used everything in preaching.
Although observing your activities with their very eyes,

those who are blind like owls and other creatures of the night
could not see your true purpose.

(7) *āuliyā-sahajiyā ki bujhibe tāhā*
     gaḍḍalikā naiyāyika bujhi pāre kāṅhā

āuliyā-sahajiyā – the bogus Āula and Sahajiyā sects; *ki* – what; *bujhibe* – will be
understood; *tāhā* – that; *gaḍḍalikā* – blindly following sheeplike people; *naiyāyika*
– logicians; *bujhi* – understand; *pāre* – able; *kāṅhā* – to what extent?

> What will the Āuls and the Sahajiyās
>> and other deviant groups ever understand?
> And what will the sheeplike common people
>> or the dry logicians ever understand?

(8) *jīvera darada-duḥkhī śrīla prabhupāda!*
     viraha-vāsare tava heri avasāda

jīvera – of the conditioned souls; *darada* – pain; *duḥkhī* – he who suffers; *śrīla prabhupāda*
– O Śrīla Bhaktisiddhānta Sarasvatī Prabhupāda; *viraha-vāsare* – on the anniversary of
the day of separation; *tava* – your; *heri* – I behold; *avasāda* – loss of spirit.

> O Śrīla Prabhupāda! You personally suffer
>> to see the suffering of the fallen conditioned souls.
> On this day of your separation
>> I am utterly despondent.

Aṣṭama Aṣṭaka
Eighth Octet

If Only You Would Come Again

(1)   *caitanyera sevā nahe nirjana bhajane*
      bujhāile bāra bāra tava nija-jane

caitanyera – of Lord Caitanya; *sevā* – service; *nahe* – not; *nirjana bhajane* – in solitary worship; *bujhāile* – tried to make understand; *bāra bāra* – again and again; *tava* – your; *nija* – own; *jane* – to the disciples.

> Lord Caitanya's method of devotional service
> is not performed by solitary worship.
> You stressed this point again and again
> when training your disciples.

(2)   *jagāi-mādhāi uddhāri' prabhu dayā kare*
      sei se-pracāra kārya bujhāle sabāre

jagāi-mādhāi – the rogues named Jagai and Madhai; *uddhāri'* – delivering; *prabhu* – Lord Caitanya; *dayā kare* – showing mercy; *sei se* – just like that; *pracāra* – preaching; *kārya* – work; *bujhāle* – made to understand; *sabāre* – to everyone.

> You explained to us all
> that our preaching method is in the mood
> of Lord Caitanya when He showed mercy
> to deliver the rascals Jagāi and Mādhāi.

(3)   *jagat bhariyā geche jagāi-mādhāi*
      sabā-i heriche bāṭa caitanya-nitāi

jagat – the world; *bhariyā* – filling up; *geche* – has gone; *jagāi-mādhāi* – Jagai and Madhai; *sabā-i* – indeed everyone; *heriche* – is looking; *bāṭa* – to the path; *caitanya-nitāi* – of Lord Caitanya and Lord Nityānanda.

> The world has now filled up
> with many Jagāis and Mādhāis to deliver.

Everyone is anxiously awaiting
the arrival of Caitanya-Nitāi's mercy.

(4)   *hena kāle tumi yadi ābāra āsite*
punar-bāra sei-bhāve kīrtana gāhite

hena – such as this; *kāle* – at the time; *tumi* – you; *yadi* – if; *ābāra* – once again; *āsite* – to come; *punaḥ-bāra* – again; *sei-bhāve* – in that way; *kīrtana* – chanting; *gāhite* – to sing.

If, at such times as these,
you were personally to return to this world,
once more chanting the holy names and preaching
in the same merciful mood of the Lord . . .

(5)   *punaḥ yadi dik-digante pracāra haita*
ānande loka saba ha'ta uchalita

punaḥ – again; *yadi* – if; *dik-digante* – in all directions; *pracāra* – preaching; *haita* – were to be; *ānande* – in bliss; *loka* – the people; *saba* – all; *ha'ta* – to become; *uchalita* – stirred up.

and if there were enthusiastic preaching activities
again taking place in every direction,
then all the people, as before,
would be stirred up in blissful excitement.

(6)   *gambhīra huṅkāre tava pāṣaṇḍī pālā'ta*
caitanya-kathāya jīvera hṛdaya bharita

gambhīra – deep; *huṅkāre* – by the roaring; *tava* – your; *pāṣaṇḍī* – atheists; *pālā'ta* – were to chase away; *caitanya-kathāya* – in the topics of Lord Caitanya; *jīvera* – of the fallen souls; *hṛdaya* – the hearts; *bharita* – were to be filled.

Your profound roaring would cause
demons and atheists to flee,
and your narrations of Lord Caitanya's message
would fill the hearts of sincere souls.

(7) *punaḥ pṛthivīte saba paḍe' yeta sāḍā*
tomāra virahe āja saba maṇi-hārā

punaḥ – again; *pṛthivīte* – on the earth; *saba* – all; *paḍe' yeta* – which; *sāḍā* – hubbub of excitement; *tomāra* – your; *virahe* – in separation; *āja* – today; *saba* – all; *maṇi-hārā* – aggrieved upon losing the most precious treasure or beloved person.

Again the whole world would be
excitedly bustling with good tidings.
But now, in your absence, everyone is mourning
the loss of the most precious treasure.

(8) *jīvera darada-duḥkhī śrīla prabhupāda!*
viraha-vāsare tava heri avasāda

jīvera – of the conditioned souls; *darada* – pain; *duḥkhī* – he who suffers; *śrīla prabhupāda* – O Śrīla Bhaktisiddhānta Sarasvatī Prabhupāda; *viraha-vāsare* – on the anniversary of the day of separation; *tava* – your; *heri* – I behold; *avasāda* – loss of spirit.

O Śrīla Prabhupāda! You personally suffer
to see the suffering of the fallen conditioned souls.
On this day of your separation
I am utterly despondent.

(9) *tomāra virahe prabhu! vidare hṛdaya*
viraha-vedanā kichu prakāśe abhaya

tomāra – your; *virahe* – in separation; *prabhu* – O master; *vidare* – splitting; *hṛdaya* – my heart; *viraha* – of separation; *vedanā* – sorrow; *kichu* – something; *prakāśe* – revealed; *abhaya* – Abhay Charanaravinda Das.

O Master! In your absence,
my heart is broken.
Abhay is hereby revealing only a small glimpse
of his wretched sorrow in separation.

—*dīna hīna kāṅgāla* / Śrī Abhaya Caraṇa (Bhaktivedānta)

Vaiśiṣṭyāṣṭaka

Vaiśiṣṭyāṣṭaka

"Eight Prayers Glorifying
the Distinctive Characteristics
of My Spiritual Master"
composed in 1961 by
His Divine Grace A. C. Bhaktivedanta Swami Prabhupāda

INTRODUCTION

On September 17, 1959, Abhay Charanaravinda Bhaktivedanta took *sannyāsa* from his godbrother, Śrī Śrīmad Bhakti-prajñāna Keśava Mahārāja, at the Keśavajī Gauḍīya Maṭha in Mathurā. He became formally known as Śrī Bhaktivedanta Swami Mahārāja. Thereafter he made a short preaching tour of Agra, Kanpur, Jhansi, and Delhi. He then returned to his quarters at the Vaṁśī-Gopālajī temple in Vṛndāvana. Early in 1960 he acquired a room at the Rādhā-Kṛṣṇa temple in the Chippiwada neighborhood of Delhi, where he wrote his first book, *Easy Journey to Other Planets.* He published it in the fall.

In February of 1961, on Vyāsa-pūjā day, the anniversary of the appearance of Śrīla Bhaktisiddhānta Sarasvatī, Bhaktivedanta Swami was again in Vṛndāvana. Some of Śrīla Bhaktisiddhānta's disciples had gathered there, offered flowers before their spiritual master's picture, and held congregational chanting. But Bhaktivedanta Swami thought that they should be doing much more than that; they should be planning and executing the worldwide preaching mission that Bhaktisiddhānta Sarasvatī had desired. Instead, they were a gathering of independent individuals, each with his own small idea, each maintaining a small center or living at someone else's center, but with no world programs, not even a program for India. Many of them had no plans or vision beyond their own bodily maintenance. Bhaktisiddhānta Sarasvatī had asked for a governing body to conduct his movement, but there was no governing body, and practically there was no movement. Some who had fought bitterly were again on speaking terms and now feared that any sudden organizational attempts might simply stir up old animosities. At least they could gather together in a civilized fashion and make an offering to their spiritual master.

Among his godbrothers, Bhaktivedanta Swami was a junior *sannyāsī*. Although a recognized writer and editor, he had no temple or followers of his own. Yet he knew he was trying to follow Bhaktisiddhānta Sarasvatī. He felt himself helpless and alone against the vast forces of *māyā*. His godbrothers were not an army united against *māyā's* forces, but were more like apathetic monks, growing old, holding on to religious principles and rituals, devoid of life. How could they gather to worship their spiritual master without remorsefully admitting their failure and, in the spirit of "better late than never," trying to rectify it?

Since the custom on Vyāsa-pūjā day was for each disciple to write an offering glorifying his spiritual master and to share it within the assembly of godbrothers, Bhaktivedanta Swami wrote an offering in Bengali poetry – more like an outburst than a tribute – and presented it before his godbrothers for their response. As he read the poem, its truth exploding in the midst of the gathering of aging *sannyāsīs*, some agreed with him, and others were incensed.

Their meeting, however, took no new direction; they did not sit down together and plan as he had pleaded. "Swami Mahārāja's" poem was taken as just another poetic expression or opinion. The godbrothers were inclined to let the old wounds heal with the passing of time. To go back over the whole thing again and reconstruct the mission as it had been before, when Śrīla Bhaktisiddhānta Sarasvatī had been present, and to attempt all those ambitious programs – how was it possible? They were getting old. Some did not want to leave the shelter of Vṛndāvana. They would worship Bhaktisiddhānta Sarasvatī within the holy *dhāma*. If Bhaktivedanta Swami could do something more, let him go ahead and try.

Bhaktivedanta Swami returned to his quarters in Keśi-ghāṭa, in deep reflection. For many years in the past he had been unable to take a leading part in the mission because of family commitments. In 1935, his godbrothers in Bombay had even asked him to be the president of the *maṭha* there, but Bhaktisiddhānta Sarasvatī had said that it was not necessary that Abhay Charan join them; he would come in his own way and do everything. Now, by the grace of his spiritual master, he was ready to fulfill the meaning of *sannyāsa*. The Kṛṣṇa conscious world he had described in his poem was not some utopia, presented merely to incite his godbrothers, a dreamer's talk of the impossible. It was possible. He personally had to write and print Kṛṣṇa conscious books and preach abroad. It was what Śrīla Bhaktisiddhānta Sarasvatī wanted. If his godbrothers would not do it cooperatively, then he would do it alone.

HEADINGS OF THE "DISTINCTIONS"

133

1 ~ Characteristics of True Renunciation

2 ~ Revolutionary Preaching in Public Places

3 ~ Serving the Message instead of Imitating the Guru

4 ~ Engaging in Preaching instead of Politics

5 ~ Returning Your Wealth to Kṛṣṇa

6 ~ The Degraded Symptoms of Kali-yuga

7 ~ The Merciful Qualities of a True Vaiṣṇava

8 ~ A Kṛṣṇa Conscious Kingdom on Earth

Vaiśiṣṭyāṣṭaka

"Eight Prayers Glorifying the Distinctive Characteristics of My Spiritual Master"

Prathama Vaiśiṣṭya
First Distinction

Characteristics of True Renunciation

(1)   *se-dina virahe prabhu! kariyāchi kheda*
      asahya hayeche yei śrī-guru-viccheda

se-dina – that day; *virahe* – in separation; *prabhu* – O master; *kariyāchi kheda* – I lamented; *asahya* – intolerable; *hayeche* – became; *yei* – which; *śrī-guru-viccheda* – cut off from the divine spiritual master.

On that fateful day of your disappearance,
    O Master, I sorrowfully mourned
in separation from my beloved *śrī-guru*.
    The disunion was intolerable.

(2)   *ājikāra śubha-dine pūjibāra tare*
      enechi añjali ei pāda-padma sma're

ājikāra – today; *śubha-dine* – on the auspicious day; *pūjibāra tare* – to worship; *enechi* – I have brought; *añjali* – palmful [an offering]; *ei* – this; *pāda-padma* – lotus feet; *sma're* – in remembrance.

To worship you on this auspicious
    anniversary day, I have brought
a humble offering of poetry
    in remembrance of your lotus feet.

(3)   *(mahā) prabhura vicāra saba vairāgya-pradhāna*
      athaca karite ha'be sabākāre dāna

(*mahā*) *prabhura* – of Śrī Caitanya Mahāprabhu; *vicāra* – the judgment; *saba* – all; *vairāgya* – renunciation; *pradhāna* – foremost; *athaca* – at the same time; *karite* – to do; *ha'be* – will be; *sabākāre* – unto everyone; *dāna* – distribution.

> Śrī Caitanya Mahāprabhu's verdict is that
> renunciation is the most important thing.
> Not only that, but knowledge of renunciation
> must be delivered to everyone.

(4) *kaniṣṭhera adhikāre nahe samādhāna*
  mahā-bhāgavata tumi diyecha sandhāna

kaniṣṭhera – of the beginner; *adhikāre* – by qualification; *nahe* – not; *samādhāna* – solution; *mahā-bhāgavata* – topmost devotee; *tumi* – you; *diyecha* – you have given; *sandhāna* – direction.

> The neophytes have no qualification
> to perform this preaching work.
> But you are an empowered devotee of the highest order,
> and you have given us clear instructions.

(5) *ajñāne mohita yārā kisera vairāgī?*
  phalgu-vairāgī tārā bāhirete tyāgī

ajñāne – by ignorance; *mohita* – bewildered; *yārā* – of whom; *kisera* – in what way; *vairāgī* – a renunciant; *phalgu-vairāgī* – a superficial renunciant; *tārā* – their; *bāhirete* – externally; *tyāgī* – a renunciant.

> If neophyte devotees are bewildered by a lack of conclusive knowledge,
> what kind of renunciants can they be?
> They will be only imitation renunciants, externally giving up things
> while internally remaining attached.

(6) *aprākṛta anubhave haya se vairāgya*
  anubhava vinā sei "śo-baṭal" ākhya

aprākṛta – transcendental; *anubhave* – by realization; *haya* – there is; *se* – that; *vairāgya* – renunciation; *anubhava* – realization; *vinā* – without; *sei* – that; *śo-baṭal* – show-bottle; *ākhya* – known as.

True renunciation is the actual result
of genuine transcendental realization.
Without such realization, simply a display of renunciation
is known as show-bottle *vairāgya*.

(7) *āra-eka "śo-baṭal" pracārera tare*
prabhura sannyāsa yei māyāvādī hāre

āra – furthermore; *eka* – one; *śo-baṭal* – show-bottle; *pracārera tare* – for the purpose of preaching; *prabhura* – of Caitanya Mahāprabhu; *sannyāsa* – the renounced order; *yei* – by which; *māyāvādī* – the impersonalists; *hāre* – are conquered.

But there is another type of show-bottle renunciation
used for the purpose of preaching.
That is Lord Caitanya's acceptance of the *sannyāsa āśrama*,
by which the Māyāvādīs are defeated.

(8) *varṇāśrama-atīta sei caitanyera vāṇī*
bhāgavata-dharma sei kaitavera hāni

varṇāśrama-atīta – transcendental to *varṇāśrama*; *sei* – that; *caitanyera vāṇī* – the teachings of Lord Caitanya; *bhāgavata-dharma* – God consciousness; *sei* – that; *kaitavera* – of cheating; *hāni* – the end.

Lord Caitanya's philosophy is far beyond
the concepts of *varṇāśrama-dharma*.
It is called *bhāgavata-dharma*, and is meant for putting an end
to all cheating processes of religion.

(9) *śuṣka-vairāgya ka're habe nā pracāra*
yukta-vairāgya-i haya sarva-sārātsāra

śuṣka – dry; *vairāgya* – renunciation; *ka're* – doing; *habe* – will be; *nā* – not; *pracāra* – preaching; *yukta-vairāgya* – appropriate renunciation; *i* – verily; *haya* – is; *sarva* – of all; *sārātsāra* – the superlative essence.

Preaching cannot be successful
    by performing dry renunciation.
Therefore *yukta-vairāgya*, appropriate renunciation,
    is the topmost essence of Lord Caitanya's teachings.

(10)   *"tomāra pradatta sannyāsa" bhaktite pracāra*
    pāṣaṇḍa bhogīra dala bujhite nācāra

tomāra – your; *pradatta* – given; *sannyāsa* – renounced order; *bhaktite* – in devotion; *pracāra* – preaching; *pāṣaṇḍa* – demonic; *bhogīra* – of the sense gratifiers; *dala* – the group; *bujhite* – to understand; *nācāra* – having no means.

The *sannyāsa* initiation you have given us
    is meant for preaching in devotion to the Lord.
Only sinful sense enjoyers
    are unable to understand this simple fact.

Vaiśiṣṭyāṣṭaka

Dvitīya Vaiśiṣṭya
Second Distinction

Revolutionary Preaching in Public Places

(1) *sannyāsa kariyā thāke parvata-gahvare*
tumi prabhu! rākha tāre harmyera marmare

sannyāsa kariyā – taking vows of renunciation; *thāke* – staying; *parvata* – of mountains; *gahvare* – in caves; *tumi* – you; *prabhu* – master; *rākha* – keep; *tāre* – them; *harmyera* – of mansions; *marmare* – in marble.

A *sannyāsī* traditionally renounces everything of the world
and goes off to live in mountain caves.
But you, O Master, keep your *sannyāsīs*
in luxurious marble mansions.

(2) *viṣayīra darśane haya viṣera bhakṣaṇa*
tumi prabhu! "lāṭa"-"vilāṭe" dāo daraśana

viṣayīra – of sense gratifiers; *darśane* – by seeing; *haya* – it is; *viṣera* – of poison; *bhakṣaṇa* – drinking; *tumi* – you; *prabhu* – O master; *lāṭa-vilāṭe* – to British governors of Indian provinces; *dāo* – you give; *daraśana* – view of yourself.

A renunciant is traditionally forbidden
to look upon a sense enjoyer,
for that is like drinking poison;
but you, O Master, deliberately visit
British governors of Indian provinces
just to give them your *darśana*.

(3) *hindura mandire mānā mleccha-yavane*
sabhā-pati ka're tāre vasāo sadane

hindura – of the Hindus; *mandire* – in the temple; *mānā* – forbidden; *mleccha-yavane* – meat-eaters and Muslims; *sabhā-pati* – chairman; *ka're* – making; *tāre* – them; *vasāo* – you seat; *sadane* – in the assembly.

The *mlecchas*, or meat-eaters, and *yāvanas*, or Muslims,
    are traditionally forbidden to enter Hindu temples,
yet you honor them as chairmen of the board
    and seat them prominently in the assembly of devotees.

(4)   *samudrera pāre yāoyā niṣedha hindure*
    tumi kintu pāṭhāo bhakta tāra-o o-pāre

samudrera pāre – beyond the ocean; *yāoyā* – causing to travel; *niṣedha* – forbidden; *hindure* – for the Hindus; *tumi* – you; *kintu* – but; *pāṭhāo* – you send; *bhakta* – devotees; *tāra-o* – of it [the ocean]; *o-pāre* – beyond.

Hindus are traditionally forbidden
    to travel across the ocean;
but boldly you send your devotees overseas,
    to preach there on your behalf.

(5)   *kalira śahara "mānā" guru-upadeśa*
    tumi kintu thāka sethā aśeṣa-viśeṣa

kalira – of Kali-yuga; *śahara* – city; *mānā* – forbidden; *guru-upadeśa* – teachings of the *ācāryas*; *tumi* – you; *kintu* – but; *thāka* – you stay; *sethā* – there; *aśeṣa-viśeṣa* – perpetually.

In the horrible cities corrupted by Kali-yuga,
    the instructions of bona-fide spiritual preceptors
are considered taboo by the populace,
    but you intentionally spend all your time there.

(6)   *nirjane cāhila bhakta gophā karibāre*
    svīkāra nahila tāhā tomāra vicāre

nirjane – in seclusion; *cāhila* – desired; *bhakta* – the devotees; *gophā* – hide; *karibāre* – to do; *svīkāra* – acceptance; *nahila* – have not; *tāhā* – that; *tomāra* – your; *vicāre* – in judgement.

Some devotees want to hide in a secluded place
    to quietly perform confidential *bhajana*,

but in your view such selfish behavior
is totally unacceptable.

(7) *ye-khānete loka-saṅgha beśī parimāṇe*
tomāra pracāra-kārya dekhita' se-khāne

ye-khānete – at which place; *loka-saṅgha* – assembly of people; *beśī* – very much;
parimāṇe – in measurement; *tomāra* – your; *pracāra-kārya* – activities of preaching;
dekhita' – is visible; *se-khāne* – at that place.

Wherever there are
the densest populations,
your preaching activities
are most visibly present.

(8) *laṇḍanete "chātrāvāsa" karibāre cāo*
paripāṭi yāte haya se kathā bujhāo

laṇḍanete – in London; *chātrāvāsa* – youth hostel; *karibāre* – to make; *cāo* – you want;
paripāṭi – orderly arrangement; *yāte* – by which; *haya* – is; *se kathā* – that topic; *bujhāo*
– you make known.

In London you want to make
a youth hostel for travelers.
You explain that it must be organized
in a first-class manner.

(9) *mleccha-deśe "chātrāvāsa" hari-kathā-tare*
e saba marmera kathā ke bujhite pāre

mleccha-deśe – in the land of meat-eaters; *chātrāvāsa* – youth hostel; *hari-kathā-tare*
– for the purpose of discussions on Lord Hari; *e* – this; *saba* – all; *marmera* – of the
meaning; *kathā* – topic; *ke* – who; *bujhite* – to understand; *pāre* – is able.

In the land of meat-eating barbarians,
a student hostel for preaching *hari-kathā*!
Who can possibly comprehend
the significance of these things?

(10)   *e saba viruddha artha samādhāna karā*
   khelā nahe hetuḍera "na" kaḍā "cha" kaḍā

e – this; *saba* – all; *viruddha* – contradictory; *artha* – meaning; *samādhāna* – solution; *karā* – to do; *khelā* – act of trifling; *nahe* – not; *hetuḍera* – of a charlatan; *na kaḍā cha kaḍā* – petty and careless handling.

The reconciliation of all these
   apparently contradictory policies
is not for the entertainment
   of foolish speculators.

Tṛtīya Vaiśiṣṭya
Third Distinction

Serving the Message instead of Imitating the Guru

(1)   *sabā-i miliyā vasi' yadi cintā kare*
      tabe-i sucāru haya se-saba pracāre

sabā-i – verily all; *miliyā* – gathering together; *vasi'* – sitting; *yadi* – if; *cintā kare* – giving consideration; *tabe-i* – verily then; *su-cāru* – very beautiful; *haya* – is; *se-saba* – all that; *pracāre* – by preaching.

[O Master!] If all your disciples sat together
    and discussed the possibilities,
then your movement would become beautified
    by all sorts of preaching programs.

(2)   *tāi se tomāra ājñā sabāi miliyā*
      pracāryera kārya-karā vāṇīte majiyā

tāi – verily; *se* – that; *tomāra* – your; *ājñā* – command; *sabāi* – everyone; *miliyā* – gathering together; *pracāryera* – of preaching; *kārya* – the work; *karā* – should perform; *vāṇīte* – in the words; *majiyā* – being absorbed.

This very thing was your explicit order for us:
    that everyone should work together
to enact the preaching mission
    while remaining immersed in your instructions.

(3)   *nakala karite gele viparīta phala*
      yata-dina yābe saba haibe vikala

nakala – imitation; *karite* – to do; *gele* – upon going; *viparīta* – opposite; *phala* – result; *yata-dina* – as many days; *yābe* – will continue; *saba* – all; *haibe* – will be; *vikala* – failure.

But if everyone simply imitates your exalted position,
> the effect is verily the opposite.
As long as this pretense continues,
> there will be only utter failure.

(4)   *ekhana-o phiriyā eso prabhura ājñāya*
      sakale miliyā maje tāṅhāra pūjāya

ekhana-o – even now; *phiriyā* – returning; *eso* – you come; *prabhura* – of our spiritual master; *ājñāya* – by the order; *sakale* – everyone; *miliyā* – gathering; *maje* – immersed; *tāṅhāra* – his; *pūjāya* – in the worship on his Vyāsa-pūjā day.

Even now, O godbrothers, you have returned here
> on the order of our spiritual master;
together we are absorbed in worshiping His Divine Grace
> on his annual Vyāsa-pūjā day.

(5)   *phula-phala-mahotsava pūjā nāhi haya*
      vāṇīra sevaka yei sei ta pūjaya

phula-phala – flowers and fruit; *mahā-utsava* – grand festival; *pūjā* – worship; *nāhi haya* – is not; *vāṇīra* – of the instructions; *sevaka* – the servant; *yei* – who; *sei* – he; *ta* – therefore; *pūjaya* – performs worship.

But merely having a festival of flowers and fruits
> does not constitute worship.
Those who serve the instructions of the spiritual master
> actually worship him.

(6)   *vāṇīra ye sevā haya sei śabda-brahma*
      phiriyā āisa bhai nā kariha dambha

vāṇīra – of the instructions; *ye* – which; *sevā* – service; *haya* – is; *sei* – that; *śabda-brahma* – transcendental sound; *phiriyā* – returning; *āisa* – please come; *bhāi* – O godbrothers; *nā* – do not; *kariha* – being such; *dambha* – proud.

In serving the spiritual master's instructions
    the disciples are empowered
    by his transcendental sound vibration.
O godbrothers, please give up your false pride
    and return to this standard.

(7)   *"kālīdāsa nāga" sei māṣṭāra maśāya*
        balechila eka-dina prakāśya sabhāya

kālīdāsa nāga – the person named Kālīdāsa Nāga [a Bengali professor at Calcutta University (1930–80), who was defeated in debate by Bhaktisiddhānta Sarasvatī and later became his disciple]; *sei* – he; *māṣṭāra* – master; *maśāya* – the learned man; *balechila* – had said; *eka-dina* – one day; *prakāśya* – openly; *sabhāya* – in the assembly.

Once the greatly learned scholar
    known as Dr. Kālīdāsa Nāga
    openly challenged our master
    in a public assembly by saying:

(8)   *kalira miśana ha'la sārā pṛthvī juḍe*
        mahāprabhura sāra-kathā khāṅcāra bhitare?

kalira – of the personality of Kali-yuga; *miśana* – the mission; *ha'la* – has been; *sārā pṛthvī* – the whole world; *juḍe* – spreads; *mahāprabhura* – of Lord Caitanya; *sāra-kathā* – essential message; *khāṅcāra* – of a cage; *bhitare* – within.

"The degraded mission of Kali-yuga
    is spreading like a plague all over the world.
Why, then, is the vital message of Lord Caitanya Mahāprabhu
    being kept locked up in a cage?"

(9)   *chiḥ! chiḥ! loka-lajjā nāi āmādera bhai*
        vyavasā-dārī cāle kari śiṣyera baḍāi

chiḥ chiḥ – shame, shame; *loka-lajjā* – public disgrace; *nāi* – not; *āmādera* – our; *bhai* – O godbrothers; *vyavasā-dārī* – businessmen; *cāle* – in a deceptive manner; *kari* – doing; *śiṣyera* – of disciples; *baḍāi* – increase.

Oh, shame! Shame! My dear godbrothers,
>   are we not embarrassed by what we are doing?
In the deceptive manner of mundane businessmen
>   we ambitiously increase the number of our own disciples.

(10)   *prabhu tāi ba'lechila pracāra karibāre*
>   *kaniṣṭha ḍhukuka śudhu ghaṇṭā nāḍibāre*

prabhu – our spiritual master; *tāi* – indeed; *ba'lechila* – had said; *pracāra* – preaching; *karibāre* – to engage in; *kaniṣṭha* – neophytes; *ḍhukuka* – may remain inside; *śudhu* – simply; *ghaṇṭā* – bell; *nāḍibāre* – to ring.

Our spiritual master has commanded us
>   to go out and preach.
Let the neophytes remain inside the temples
>   and simply ring the bells.

Caturtha Vaiśiṣṭya
Fourth Distinction

Engaging in Preaching instead of Politics

(1) *e saba nahe prabhura pracārera rīti*
     e saba kareche guru-goṅsāira jāti

e saba – all this; *nahe* – is not; *prabhura* – of our master; *pracārera* – of preaching; *rīti* – method; *e saba* – all this; *kareche* – is done; *guru-goṅsāira jāti* – of the caste *gosvāmīs*, who pretend to be *gurus*.

> All these new things that we have fabricated
> > are not our spiritual master's preaching methods.
> This charade of posing as **gurus**
> > is the business of deviant caste **gosvāmīs**.

(2) *kintu ceye dekha kibā durdaśā hayeche*
     viṣayī haiyā sabe pracāra cheḍeche

kintu – but; *ceye dekha* – just see; *kibā* – how much; *durdaśā* – calamity; *hayeche* – has arisen; *viṣayī* – sense gratifier; *haiyā* – becoming; *sabe* – by everyone; *pracāra* – preaching; *cheḍeche* – has abandoned.

> Just open your eyes and see
> > the tragedy that has arisen.
> Everyone has become a sense enjoyer
> > and given up preaching.

(3) *mandire-o tālā-bandha hayeche ārambha*
     bhāgavata pracāra kara, nā kara vilambha

mandire-o – even in the temples; *tālā-bandha* – locked with padlocks; *hayeche* – have been; *ārambha* – beginning; *bhāgavata pracāra* – preaching on the Lord's behalf; *kara* – please do; *nā* – do not; *kara* – do; *vilambha* – hesitation.

In your temples you have even begun
to padlock the doors.
Oh, just preach our *bhāgavata-dharma.*
Don't procrastinate any longer!

(4) *medinīra madhye āche ekaṭi medinī*
kiṁvā śabda yāya tava asama bhedinī

medinīra – of the earth; *madhye* – within; *āche* – there is; *ekaṭi* – one; *medinī* – earth; *kiṁvā* – or; *śabda* – sound; *yāya* – goes; *tava* – your; *asama* – dissimilar; *bhedinī* – that which penetrates.

Within this very world of matter
there is another hidden world of spiritual potency.
Your utterance of transcendental sound vibration, however,
penetrates the veil between these two different realms.

(5) *"mallāra dauḍa tāi masjida paryanta"*
e-saba pracāra-kārya āji kara anta

mallāra – of the Muslim mullah, or priest; *dauḍa* – the limit; *tāi* – just so; *masjida* – the mosque; *paryanta* – the extent; *e-saba* – all this; *pracāra-kārya* – activities of preaching; *āji* – today; *kara* – make; *anta* – finish.

It is said: "The Muslim mullah
ventures no further than the walls of the mosque."
All preaching that is limited by such concepts
should be put to an end this very day.

(6) *ā-samudra medinī-pāra brahmāṇḍa-bhedinī*
sakale miliyā kara pracāra-vāhinī

ā-samudra – to the sea; *medinī-pāra* – across the earth; *brahmā-aṇḍa-bhedinī* – penetrating the shell of Lord Brahmā's egglike universe; *sakale* – everyone; *miliyā* – gathering together; *kara* – do; *pracāra-vāhinī* – the river of preaching.

All of us should unite in purpose and flood the lands
with waves of Kṛṣṇa conscious preaching,

crossing oceans, covering the world,
    penetrating the universal shell.

(7)   *tabe se prabhura pūjāra habe paripāṭi*
      āja-i pratijñā kara chāḍa kuṭi-nāṭi

tabe – then; *se* – that; *prabhura* – of our master; *pūjāra* – by the worship of the annual Vyāsa-pūjā ceremony; *habe* – will be; *paripāṭi* – orderly arrangement; *āja-i* – verily today; *pratijñā* – promise; *kara* – please make; *chāḍa* – please give up; *kuṭi-nāṭi* – trivial hair-splitting.

If we do so, this annual ceremony of worshiping
    our *guru* on his Vyāsa-pūjā day will properly honor him.
Oh, please, make a pledge on this very day
    to give up all petty fault-finding.

(8)   *āja-i ekatra haye karaha mantavya*
      pāñce mili vicāraha ki karā kartavya

āja-i – verily today; *ekatra* – in one place; *haye* – being; *karaha* – please do; *mantavya* – input; *pāñce* – in council; *mili* – together; *vicāraha* – please consider; *ki karā* – what to accomplish; *kartavya* – what should be done.

Everyone, since we are together on this day,
    please contribute your valuable perspective.
All of us can meet to discuss the situation
    and together decide what should be done.

(9)   *tyāgī haiyācha bhāi, kara sabe tyāga*
      "vāṇī"-tyāga kara yadi kisera virāga?

tyāgī – renunciants; *haiyācha* – you have become; *bhāi* – O godbrothers; *kara* – please do; *sabe* – everything; *tyāga* – renounce; *vāṇī* – the instructions of the *guru*; *tyāga* – renounce; *kara* – please do; *yadi* – if; *kisera* – what type; *virāga* – renunciation.

You have become renunciants, O godbrothers,
    so indeed renounce everything.

But if you also give up your spiritual master's order,
what kind of renunciation is that?

(10)   *"guru-bhogī," "guru-tyāgī" dui ta' asāra*
         "guru-sevī" hale para bujhibe vicāra

guru-bhogī – those who use the spiritual master's mission for their sense gratification;
guru-tyāgī – those who reject the spiritual master by trying to become the spiritual
master; *dui* – both; *ta'* – thus; *asāra* – useless; *guru-sevī* – one who serves the *guru*;
hale – becoming; *para* – upon; *bujhibe* – will understand; *vicāra* – the proper conclusion.

There are two kinds of worthless disciples:
    those who try to enjoy their master's assets (**guru-bhogī**)
    and those who reject their master's authority (**guru-tyāgī**).
Only those disciples who serve their spiritual master (**guru-sevī**)
    will know what they should do.

Pañcama Vaiśiṣṭya
Fifth Distinction

Returning Your Wealth to Kṛṣṇa

(1)   *ekalā īśvara haye yadi dhana bāḍe*
    jaḍera pratiṣṭhā sei sādhu tāhā chāḍe

ekalā – one; *īśvara* – controller; *haye* – since there is; *yadi* – if; *dhana* – wealth; *bāḍe* – increases; *jaḍera* – of matter; *pratiṣṭhā* – position of false materialistic pride; *sei* – that; *sādhu* – saintly person; *tāhā* – that; *chāḍe* – gives up.

The devotee knows that the Supreme Lord is the only enjoyer.
Therefore, if his personal opulence increases,
a saintly person rejects the false prestige of
mundane profit, adoration, and distinction.

(2)   *tomāra kanaka bhāi bhogera janaka*
    prabhupāda balechena se-kathā athaka

tomāra – your; *kanaka* – gold; *bhāi* – O godbrothers; *bhogera* – of sense gratification; *janaka* – the cause; *prabhupāda* – O Śrīla Bhaktisiddhānta Sarasvatī Prabhupāda; *balechena* – had spoken; *se-kathā* – that statement; *athaka* – hereafter.

Your hoarding of money, O godbrothers,
is the cause of material sense enjoyment.
Śrīla Prabhupāda himself warned you
to avoid this danger.

(3)   *tomāra sampatti chāḍa pracārera tare*
    ekatre vasiyā kara viśeṣa vicāre

tomāra – your; *sampatti* – opulence; *chāḍa* – please give up; *pracārera tare* – for the purpose of preaching; *ekatre* – in one place; *vasiyā* – sitting; *kara* – please do; *viśeṣa* – special; *vicāre* – in discussion.

Just give up your personal fortunes
for the cause of preaching;
sit together and make a special effort
to plan for their practical use.

(4) *svayaṁ bhagavān kahe ekalā āmāra*
nāhi bala sabe mili karaha pracāra

svayam – Himself; *bhagavān* – the Supreme Lord; *kahe* – says; *ekalā* – alone; *āmāra* –
Mine; *nāhi* – do not; *bala* – speak; *sabe* – everyone; *mili* – together; *karaha* – please do;
pracāra – preaching.

The Supreme Lord Himself says,
"Everything is Mine alone."
Do not protest!
Just join together and preach.

(5) *prabhupāda balechena sei vāṇī śeṣa*
prayatna karaha tāhe āśeṣa-viśeṣa

prabhupāda – Śrīla Bhaktisiddhānta Sarasvatī; *balechena* – has spoken; *sei vāṇī* – these
words; *śeṣa* – final; *prayatna* – effort; *karaha* – please do; *tāhe* – in that regard; *āśeṣa-
viśeṣa* – adopting numerous and various ways.

Śrīla Prabhupāda personally gave that command
as his final instruction to us.
Please take great care to carry out his order
by adopting various preaching strategies.

(6) *anyathāya vṛthā-śrama saba paṇḍa habe*
sādhu sāvadhāna hao paścāte pastābe

anyathāya – otherwise; *vṛthā-śrama* – useless labor; *saba* – all; *paṇḍa* – spoiled; *habe* –
will become; *sādhu* – appropriate; *sāvadhāna* – careful; *hao* – please become; *paścāte* –
later; *pastābe* – will regret.

Otherwise, all your efforts are in vain.
All your results will be spoiled.
Be very careful in this regard,
or later you will regret everything.

(7)   *emana ki kaṭhina kārya ekatra milite?*
kena-i bā eta kathā hatecha balite?

emana – in this way; *ki kaṭhina* – what is difficult; *kārya* – work; *ekatra* – in one place; *milite* – in meeting; *kena-i* – indeed why; *bā* – or; *eta* – this; *kathā* – topic; *hatecha* – thus needed; *balite* – to speak.

Is it really such a difficult task for us
to come together as a united movement?
And why do all these things
even need to be said to you?

(8)   *chāḍa jida kara hita samaya ye nāi*
śubha-milibāra tithi esa saba bhāi

chāḍa – please give up; *jida* – tenacity; *kara* – please do; *hita* – beneficial; *samaya* – time; *ye* – which; *nāi* – is not; *śubha* – auspicious; *milibāra* – of meeting; *tithi* – date; *esa* – please come; *saba* – everyone; *bhāi* – O godbrothers.

Please give up stubbornness and do the right thing.
There is no time to lose!
Oh, come forth now, dear godbrothers!
This is the most auspicious occasion to unite.

Ṣaṣṭa Vaiśiṣṭya
Sixth Distinction

The Degraded Symptoms of Kali-yuga

(1)   *ghare ghare maṭha saba sthāpite ye habe*
      pṛthivīra koṇe koṇe kabe se yāibe?

ghare ghare – in each and every home; *maṭha* – temple; *saba* – all; *sthāpite* – to establish;
ye – which; *habe* – will be; *pṛthivīra* – of the earth; *koṇe koṇe* – in each and every corner;
kabe – when; *se* – that; *yāibe* – will go.

> Oh, when will that day come,
>> when a temple will be established
> in each and every home
>> in all corners of the world?

(2)   *hāi-korṭera jaja habe gauḍīya-vaiṣṇava*
      tilakera śobhā habe sabāra vaibhava

hāi-korṭera – of the high court; *jaja* – the judge; *habe* – will be; *gauḍīya-vaiṣṇava* – a
Gauḍīya Vaiṣṇava; *tilakera* – of *tilaka*; *śobhā* – splendor; *habe* – will be; *sabāra* – of all
of them; *vaibhava* – the beauty.

> When will the high court judges
>> be devout Gauḍīya Vaiṣṇavas,
> with radiant *tilaka* marks
>> beautifully decorating their foreheads?

(3)   *vaiṣṇava se bhoṭa laye rāṣṭra-pati habe*
      pracāra sarvatra bhāi prasārita habe

vaiṣṇava – a Vaiṣṇava; *se* – that; *bhoṭa* – votes; *laye* – taking; *rāṣṭra-pati* – president; *habe*
– will be; *pracāra* – preaching; *sarvatra* – everywhere; *bhāi* – O godbrothers; *prasārita* –
spreading; *habe* – will be.

> When will a Vaiṣṇava win votes from the people
>> and be elected president of the country?

And when will pure preaching, O godbrothers,
    be spread everywhere?

(4)   *bhagavānera sampatti asura luṭe khāya*
      nirīha prajā-gaṇa saba kare hāya hāya

bhagavānera – of the Lord; *sampatti* – wealth; *asura* – demons; *luṭe* – by plundering; *khāya* – enjoy; *nirīha* – innocent; *prajā-gaṇa* – populace; *saba* – all; *kare* – do; *hāya hāya* – alas, alas.

Now all the demons are simply
    plundering and enjoying the Lord's resources,
as the helpless populace cries in distress,
    "Alas! Alas!"

(5)   *asurera "plyāna" cāya tādera ṭhakāte*
      go-dhūma vikāya maṇa batriśa ṭākāte

asurera – of the demons; *plyāna* – so-called plans; *cāya* – desire; *tādera* – of them; *ṭhakāte* – swindling; *go-dhūma* – wheat flour; *vikāya* – is sold; *maṇa* – a mound (82 pounds or 37 kilos); *batriśa* – thirty-two; *ṭākāte* – by rupees.

The demons delight in concocting so many "plans"
    just to cheat the people.
They outrageously inflate the price of wheat flour
    to thirty-two rupees a mound.

(6)   *lohāra śālāra khule udara bharābe?*
      kṣudhāra tāḍane saba ghāsa-asthi khābe

lohāra – of iron; *śālāra* – of the workshop; *khule* – opening; *udara* – stomach; *bharābe* – will fill; *kṣudhāra* – of hunger; *tāḍane* – being tortured; *saba* – everyone; *ghāsa* – grass; *asthi* – pits of fruit; *khābe* – will eat.

How will building an iron factory
    fill a hungry person's belly?
Being afflicted with starvation, the people
    will be forced to eat grass and mango pits.

(7) *du'-payasāra sūtā galāya brāhmaṇa balābe*
     geruyāra poṣāka-mātra sannyāsīra habe

du'-payasāra – of two *paisā*; *sūtā* – string; *galāya* – around the neck; *brāhmaṇa* – a *brāhmaṇa*; *balābe* – will be called; *geruyāra* – of red ochre; *poṣāka* – garment; *mātra* – only; *sannyāsīra* – of a renunciant; *habe* – will be.

> By simply wearing a string costing two *paisā*,
> a man is called a *brāhmaṇa*.
> By simply wearing a cloth dyed saffron,
> another has become a *sannyāsī*.

(8) *gṛhī bhikṣā kare saba sannyāsīra kāche*
     koṭi koṭi ṭākā byāṅke sannyāsīra āche

gṛhī – householders; *bhikṣā kare* – begging for alms; *saba* – all; *sannyāsīra kāche* – from the renunciants; *koṭi koṭi* – tens of millions; *ṭākā* – rupees; *byāṅke* – in the bank; *sannyāsīra* – of the renunciants; *āche* – there is.

> The householders now beg for donations
> from all the *sannyāsīs*
> because these so-called *sannyāsīs*
> have tens of millions of rupees in the bank.

(9) *kalira prabhāva bāḍe yata-dina yāya*
     kali-hata jīva saba kare hāya hāya

kalira – of Kali-yuga; *prabhāva* – the potency; *bāḍe* – increases; *yata-dina* – as many days; *yāya* – pass; *kali-hata* – tortured by Kali-yuga; *jīva* – conditioned souls; *saba* – all; *kare* – do [exclaim]; *hāya hāya* – alas, alas.

> The pernicious influence of Kali-yuga
> increases day by day,
> as all the poor souls tortured by Kali
> cry out in distress, "Alas! Alas!"

(10) *daśa hājāra go-hatyā haya prati-dina*
      amedhya bhojana kare "līḍāra" pravīṇa

daśa hājāra – ten thousand; *go-hatyā* – killing of cows; *haya* – there is; *prati-dina* – every day; *amedhya* – unholy; *bhojana* – foodstuffs; *kare* – do [eat]; *līḍāra* – so-called leaders; *pravīṇa* – prominent.

> Ten thousand cows are killed every day
>> in slaughterhouses,
> and the nation's so-called leaders
>> are actually eating this unholy meat.

(11) *māṭiyā buddhira loka dine dine bāḍe*
      pati-patnīra samparka saba eka kathāya chāḍe

māṭiyā buddhira – of dirty intelligence; *loka* – people; *dine dine* – day by day; *bāḍe* – increase; *pati-patnīra* – of husband and wife; *samparka* – relationship; *saba* – all; *eka kathāya* – upon one talk; *chāḍe* – separate.

> People of unclean mentality
>> increase their numbers day by day.
> Husbands and wives separate forever
>> at the first unpleasant word.

(12) *piśācu hailu loku kalira prabhāve*
      loka-duḥkhī vaiṣṇavera kṛpāra abhāve

piśāca – demons; *haila* – have become; *loka* – the people; *kalira* – of Kali-yuga; *prabhāve* – by the power; *loka-duḥkhī vaiṣṇavera* – of the devotees, who are saddened by the suffering of the people; *kṛpāra* – of the mercy; *abhāve* – in the absence.

> Under the influence of the Age of Kali,
>> all people have become demons,
> being bereft of the mercy of Vaiṣṇavas,
>> who are saddened by the suffering of others.

Saptama Vaiśiṣṭya
Seventh Distinction

The Merciful Qualities of a True Vaiṣṇava

(1) *para-duḥkha-duḥkhī haya vaiṣṇava prasiddha*
     sei khyāti habe saba pracāre pravṛddha

para – other people; *duḥkha* – the sufferings; *duḥkhī* – those who also suffer; *haya* – are; *vaiṣṇava* – the devotees; *prasiddha* – famous; *sei* – that; *khyāti* – renown; *habe* – will be; *saba* – all; *pracāre* – by preaching; *pravṛddha* – the increase.

The Vaiṣṇavas are famous as *para-duḥkha-duḥkhī*,
> **for they feel great pain to witness anyone suffering.**
This renown can be justified
> **only as they increase their preaching.**

(2) *nitya-siddha kṛṣṇa-bhakti jāgile sabāra*
     āpani pālābe kali kari' hā-hā-kāra

nitya-siddha – eternally perfect; *kṛṣṇa-bhakti* – devotion to Kṛṣṇa; *jāgile* – when it awakens; *sabāra* – of everyone; *āpani* – himself; *pālābe* – will flee; *kali* – the personality of Kali; *kari'* – doing [exclaiming]; *hā-hā* – alas, alas; *kāra* – the sound.

When devotional service to Kṛṣṇa, which is eternally perfect,
> **is awakened in everyone,**
then the demonic personality of Kali will flee for his life,
> **loudly wailing, "Alas! Alas!"**

(3) *"prāṇinām upakārāya" mahāprabhu-vāṇī*
     iha-kāla-parā-kāla sukhera se khani

prāṇinām – of all living entities; *upakārāya* – for the benefit; *mahāprabhu-vāṇī* – the words of Lord Caitanya; *iha-kāla* – this life; *parā-kāla* – the next life; *sukhera* – of happiness; *se* – that; *khani* – storehouse.

Śrī Caitanya Mahāprabhu taught His followers:
> **"One must act for the benefit of all living beings."**

For a devotee, this work is the storehouse of happiness
in the present life and in the next.

(4)   *eta kāja paḍe āche tomādera hāte*
      ekatre miliyā kārya karaha tāhāte

eta – all this; *kāja* – work; *paḍe* – falls; *āche* – is; *tomādera* – of all of you; *hāte* – in the
hands; *ekatre* – together; *miliyā* – gathering together; *kārya* – work; *karaha* – please do;
tāhāte – for that very thing.

> This preaching work of the Lord
>   has been entrusted to you, O godbrothers,
> so, please, together in a unified endeavor
>   see that it is done according to the Lord's desire.

(5)   *vāsudeva vipra bale prabhure namiyā*
      sakala jīvere dāo uddhāra kariyā

vāsudeva vipra – the *brāhmaṇa* named Vāsudeva; *bale* – said; *prabhure* – to Lord Caitanya;
namiyā – bowing down; *sakala jīvere* – unto all souls; *dāo* – please give; *uddhāra kariyā*
– delivering.

> As Vāsudeva Datta said to Lord Caitanya,
>   after first bowing down before Him:
> "Please deliver all the living beings
>   from the whole material world.

(6)   *tādera saba pāpa-tāpa mo-hīnere dāo*
      duḥkhī jīvera duḥkha tumi se ghucāo

tādera – their; *saba* – all; *pāpa* – sins; *tāpa* – sufferings; *mo* – me; *hīnere* – unto the fallen
one; *dāo* – please give; *duḥkhī jīvera* – of the miserable souls; *duḥkha* – misery; *tumi* –
You; *se* – that; *ghucāo* – please relieve.

> "Just give all their sins and sufferings to me,
>   who am the most fallen.
> In this way, You may relieve all the distress
>   of the miserable conditioned souls."

(7)　*sei ta vaiṣṇava-śreṣṭha para-duḥkhe duḥkhī*
　　ātmendriya-tṛpti yāhe nahe tārā sukhī

sei – he; *ta* – indeed; *vaiṣṇava-śreṣṭha* – the best of devotees; *para-duḥkhe* – because of the suffering of others; *duḥkhī* – unhappy; *ātmā-indriya* – own senses; *tṛpti* – gratification; *yāhe* – at which; *nahe* – there is not; *tārā* – his; *sukhī* – being happy.

Vāsudeva Datta was indeed the best of Vaiṣṇavas,
　　being sad to see the suffering of others.
He knew that there was no real happiness to be found
　　in his own sense gratification.

(8)　*ki dayā karite pāre avaiṣṇava-jana!*
　　aparādhī haya mātra "daridra nārāyaṇa"!

ki dayā – what mercy; *karite* – to show; *pāre* – is possible; *avaiṣṇava-jana* – nondevotees; *aparādhī* – offender; *haya* – is; *mātra* – only; *daridra nārāyaṇa* – "poor Nārāyaṇa" [the erroneous concept popularized by Māyāvādīs, that wretched people are Lord Nārāyaṇa Himself in a poor disguise].

Can real mercy be demonstrated
　　by those who are not Vaiṣṇavas?
The swamis who supposedly show compassion to others
　　under the philosophical banner of "poor Nārāyaṇa"
are simply offenders to the Lord.

(9)　*vijñāna-sammata sei vaiṣṇavera dayā*
　　vaiṣṇava-vihīna bhūme māyā duratyayā

vijñāna – science; *sammata* – conforming to; *sei* – that; *vaiṣṇavera* – of the devotees; *dayā* – the mercy; *vaiṣṇava-vihīna* – without the devotees; *bhūme* – on earth; *māyā* – the illusory energy; *duratyayā* – very difficult to cross.

The mercy shown by the Vaiṣṇavas
　　is scientific and authorized.
Without the Vaiṣṇavas' mercy in this world,
　　the illusory energy is insurmountable.

(10) *viṣṇu-vaiṣṇava-rājya yadi dharāya haya*
  tabe-i se sukhī loka muni-ṛṣi kaya

viṣṇu-vaiṣṇava – Lord Viṣṇu and the Vaiṣṇavas; *rājya* – the kingdom; *yadi* – if; *dharāya* – on earth; *haya* – there is; *tabe-i* – verily then; *se* – that; *sukhī* – happy; *loka* – the people; *muni-ṛṣi* – the saints and sages; *kaya* – say.

If there is a kingdom of Lord Viṣṇu and the Vaiṣṇavas
established on earth,
then only will the people be happy.
This is confirmed by all the great saints and sages.

Aṣṭama Vaiśiṣṭya
Eighth Distinction

A Kṛṣṇa Conscious Kingdom on Earth

(1)   *kena loka kāṅde saba rāma-rājya tare?*
     eka-mātra kāraṇa sei viṣṇu-rājya kare

kena – why; *loka* – the people; *kāṅde* – are crying; *saba* – all; *rāma-rājya* – for the kingdom of Lord Rāma; *tare* – on behalf of; *eka-mātra* – only; *kāraṇa* – cause; *sei* – that; *viṣṇu-rājya* – the kingdom of Lord Viṣṇu; *kare* – making.

Why are all the people crying for Rāma-rājya,
     the kingdom that was personally governed by the Lord?
It can be achieved again,
     but only by establishing a God-centered nation.

(2)   *kṛṣṇa yudhiṣṭhire vasāya rāja-siṁhāsane*
     dhane-dhānye pūrṇa dharā vaiṣṇavera guṇe

kṛṣṇa – Lord Kṛṣṇa; *yudhiṣṭhire* – to King Yudhiṣṭhira; *vasāya* – seated; *rāja-siṁhāsane* – upon the royal throne; *dhane* – in riches; *dhānye* – in paddy; *pūrṇa* – full; *dharā* – the earth; *vaiṣṇavera* – of the devotee; *guṇe* – by the attributes.

Lord Kṛṣṇa personally installed King Yudhiṣṭhira
     upon the royal lion-throne.
At that time the whole world was opulent with riches and grains
     because of the auspiciousness of having a Vaiṣṇava leader.

(3)   *nada-nadī vṛkṣa-māṭha-giri bhara pūra*
     dugdhavatī gābhī dugdhe bhāsāya pracūra

nada – rivers; *nadī* – streams; *vṛkṣa* – trees; *māṭha* – grazing fields; *giri* – mountains; *bharapūra* – fully opulent; *dugdhavatī* – bearing milk; *gābhī* – the cows; *dugdhe* – with milk; *bhāsāya* – overflowing; *pracūra* – profuse.

The rivers, streams, trees, fields, and mountains
     were all bountiful with their offerings.

And the cows were overflowing
with an abundance of milk.

(4)   *paśu-pakṣī jīva-jantu hiṁsā nāhi kare*
      vaiṣṇavī rājyera vidhi prasiddha saṁsāre

paśu – animals; *pakṣī* – birds; *jīva-jantu* – lower creatures; *hiṁsā* – killing; *nāhi kare* – did
not do; *vaiṣṇavī* – devoted; *rājyera* – of the kingdom; *vidhi* – systems; *prasiddha* – famous;
saṁsāre – throughout the universe.

Even the animals, birds, and lower creatures
did not kill each other as they do now.
The quality of life in that Vaiṣṇava kingdom
was glorified throughout the universe.

(5)   *sakale ānande magna hari-guṇa gāya*
      dekhiyā vaiṣṇava hṛdaya ānande nācāya

sakale – everyone; *ānande* – in bliss; *magna* – absorbed; *hari-guṇa* – the divine qualities
of Lord Hari; *gāya* – singing; *dekhiyā* – seeing; *vaiṣṇava hṛdaya* – the hearts of the
devotees; *ānande* – in bliss; *nācāya* – causing to leap in joy.

Immersed in transcendental bliss,
everyone was singing the glories of Lord Hari.
The hearts of the Vaiṣṇavas who saw this
were leaping in ecstasy.

(6)   *kṛṣṇa-bhakti-gandha-hīna viṣaya vebhāra*
      bhariyā giyāche āja jagata saṁsāra

kṛṣṇa-bhakti – devotion to Lord Kṛṣṇa; *gandha* – a scent; *hīna* – bereft; *viṣaya* – sense
objects; *vebhāra* – intolerably miserable; *bhariyā* – filled; *giyāche* – is gone; *āja* – today;
jagata saṁsāra – the material world.

But today the entire world is filled with mundane people
devoid of even a trace of devotion to Lord Kṛṣṇa.
Instead, they are completely miserable
in contact with material sense objects.

(7) *athaca śānti tārā kare anveṣaṇa*
  pracārera dvārā tāhā karaha pūraṇa

athaca – still; *śānti* – peace; *tārā* – they; *kare anveṣaṇa* – are searching; *pracārera dvārā* – by preaching; *tāhā* – that; *karaha* – please do; *pūraṇa* – fulfillment.

> Still, even these materialistic people
> > are searching for peace of mind.
> O godbrothers! Please fulfill their desire
> > by preaching Kṛṣṇa consciousness.

(8) *ājikāra dine bhāi koṭi-baddha hao*
  pracārera dvārā hata jīvere vāñcāo

ājikāra – of today; *dine* – this very day; *bhāi* – O godbrothers; *koṭi* – either of two parties in a dispute; *baddha* – united; *hao* – you may be; *pracārera dvārā* – by means of preaching; *hata* – lost; *jīvere* – unto the souls; *vāñcāo* – may you rescue.

> On this very day of Vyāsa-pūjā, O godbrothers,
> > just reconcile your separate factions and unite.
> Come to the rescue of all the fallen souls
> > by preaching Kṛṣṇa consciousness to them.

(9) *śrīla prabhupāda! tumi āji kara dayā*
  e-bāra karuṇā kara haiyā amāyā

śrīla prabhupāda – O Śrīla Prabhupāda; *tumi* – you; *āji* – today; *kara* – please do [show]; *dayā* – mercy; *e-bāra* – this time; *karuṇā* – compassion; *kara* – please show; *haiyā* – becoming; *amāyā* – affectionate.

> O Śrīla Prabhupāda!
> > Please be merciful upon us today.
> Have compassion now
> > and let us feel your affection for us.

(10) *svatantratā yāra yata hoka jalāñjali*
  dīna "abhaya" deya āji se añjali

svatantratā – independence; *yāra* – whose; *yata* – all; *hoka* – may be; *jala-añjali* – a palmful thrown into water; *dīna* – humble; *abhaya* – Abhay Charan De; *deya* – gives; *āji* – today; *se* – this; *añjali* – offering.

> Whatever independence we may have,
> now may it be cast into the waters.
> The most fallen Abhay submits
> this humble offering today.

—Tridaṇḍī Svāmī Śrīmad Bhaktivedānta Svāmī Mahārāja

Bhagavān Kṛṣṇera
Pāda-Padme Prārthanā

Bhagavān Kṛṣṇera
Pāda-Padme Prārthanā

"Prayer to the Lotus Feet of Kṛṣṇa"
composed by His Divine Grace
A. C. Bhaktivedanta Swami Prabhupāda
aboard the *Jaladuta*, on September 13, 1965

INTRODUCTION

On Friday, September 10, 1965, at the age of sixty-nine, Bhaktivedanta Swami Mahārāja was aboard the *Jaladuta* in the middle of the Atlantic Ocean. He wrote in his diary: "Today the ship is plying very smoothly. I feel today better. But I am feeling separation of Śrī Vṛndāvana and my Lords Śrī Govinda, Gopīnātha, Rādhā-Dāmodara. My only solace is *Śrī Caitanya-caritāmṛta*, in which I am tasting the nectar of Lord Caitanya's *līlā*. I have left Bhārata-bhūmi just to execute the order of Śrī Bhaktisiddhānta Sarasvatī, in pursuance of Lord Caitanya's order. I have no qualification, but I have taken up the risk just to carry out the order of His Divine Grace. I depend fully on Their mercy so far away from Vṛndāvana." Three days later, in this mood of pure devotion, he composed a prayer in Bengali poetry.

During the voyage, as Śrīla Prabhupāda noted in his diary, he sometimes stood on deck at the ship's rail, watching the ocean and the sky and thinking of the *Caitanya-caritāmṛta*, Vṛndāvana-dhāma, and the order of his spiritual master to preach in the West. Mrs. Pandia, the captain's wife, whom Śrīla Prabhupāda considered to be "an intelligent and learned lady," foretold Śrīla Prabhupāda's future. If he were to pass beyond this crisis in his health – having suffered two heart attacks at sea – she said it would indicate the good will of Lord Kṛṣṇa.

The ocean voyage of 1965 was a calm one for the *Jaladuta*. The captain said that never in his career had he seen such a calm Atlantic crossing. Prabhupāda replied that the calmness was Lord Kṛṣṇa's mercy, and Mrs. Pandia asked Prabhupāda to come back with them so that they might have another such crossing. Śrīla Prabhupāda wrote in his diary, "If the Atlantic would have shown its usual face, perhaps I would have died. But Lord Kṛṣṇa has taken charge of the ship."

On September 13, Prabhupāda noted in his diary: "Thirty-second day of journey. Cooked *bāṭi kicharī*. It appeared to be delicious, so I was able to take some food. Today I have disclosed my mind to my companion, Lord Śrī Kṛṣṇa. There is a Bengali poem made by me in this connection."

This poem was a prayer to Lord Kṛṣṇa, and it is filled with Prabhupāda's devotional confidence in the mission that he was undertaking on behalf of his spiritual master. In the same straightforward, factual manner in which he had noted the date, the weather, and his state of health, he now described his helpless dependence on his "eternal companion," Lord Kṛṣṇa, and his absorption in the ecstasy of separation from Kṛṣṇa. He described the relationship between the spiritual master and the disciple, and he praised his own spiritual master, Śrī Śrīmad Bhaktisiddhānta Sarasvatī, by whose strong desire the holy name of Lord Gaurāṅga would be spread throughout all the countries of the Western world. He plainly stated that his spiritual master had ordered him to accomplish this mission of worldwide Kṛṣṇa consciousness, and feeling unworthy he prayed to Lord Kṛṣṇa for strength.

The last verses give a confidential glimpse into Śrīla Prabhupāda's direct relationship with Lord Kṛṣṇa. Prabhupāda called on Kṛṣṇa and longed for the joy of again wandering the cowherd pastures of Vraja. He addressed Kṛṣṇa as *bhāi*, "my dear brother." This memory of Kṛṣṇa, he wrote, came because of a great desire to serve the Lord. Externally, Śrīla Prabhupāda was experiencing great difficulty; he had been aboard a ship for a month and had suffered heart attacks and repeated seasickness. Moreover, even if he were to recover from those difficulties, his arrival in America would bring many more difficulties. But remembering the desire of his spiritual master, taking strength from reading the *Caitanya-caritāmṛta*, and revealing his mind in his prayer to Lord Kṛṣṇa, Prabhupāda remained confident in the Lord's power to use him as an instrument in preaching the sublime message of Śrī Caitanya Mahāprabhu.

Bhagavān Kṛṣṇera Pāda-Padme Prārthanā

"Prayer to the Lotus Feet of Kṛṣṇa"

[refrain:] *kṛṣṇa taba puṇya habe bhāi*
e puṇya karibe jabe,   rādhārāṇī khuśī habe,
dhruva ati boli tomā tāi

kṛṣṇa – Śrī Kṛṣṇa; *taba* – your; *puṇya* – piety; *habe* – will be; *bhāi* – O brother; *e puṇya* – pious act; *karibe* – perform; *jabe* – when; *rādhārāṇī* – Śrīmatī Rādhārāṇī; *khuśī habe* – will be pleased; *dhruva* – absolute truth; *ati* – very much; *boli* – I say; *tomā* – to you; *tāi* – therefore.

O brother, Kṛṣṇa,

I emphatically say to You

that when You perform this pious act

Śrīmatī Rādhārāṇī will be surely pleased with You

and You will achieve (great) piety.[*]

(1) *śrī-siddhānta sarasvatī,   śacī-suta priya ati,*
kṛṣṇa-sevaya yara tula nāi
sei se mahānta-guru,   jagatera madhye uru,
kṛṣṇa-bhakti deya ṭhāi ṭhāi

śrī-siddhānta sarasvatī – Śrīmad Bhaktisiddhānta Sarasvatī Ṭhākura; *śacī-suta* – the son of mother Śacī; *priya ati* – very dear; *kṛṣṇa-sevāya* – in Kṛṣṇa's service; *yāra* – whose; *tula* – comparison; *nāi* – there is not; *sei se* – that person; *mahānta-guru* – great spiritual master; *jagatera madhye* – within the universe; *uru* – magnanimous; *kṛṣṇa-bhakti* – devotional service to Kṛṣṇa; *deya* – gives; *ṭhāi ṭhāi* – at different places.

---

[*]The previous translation of the refrain was: "I emphatically say to you, O brothers, you will obtain your good fortune from the Supreme Lord Kṛṣṇa only when Śrīmatī Rādhārāṇī becomes pleased with you." The main problem with this translation, produced not by Śrīla Prabhupāda but by one of his disciples, is that it missed the point that Śrīla Prabhupāda is addressing Kṛṣṇa, not "brothers." *Kṛṣṇa taba puṇya habe bhāi* means "O brother, Kṛṣṇa, You will achieve piety." This mistake resulted in a flawed translation, which the BBT felt important to fix.

Śrī Bhaktisiddhānta Sarasvatī Ṭhākura,
> who is very dear to Lord Caitanya, the son of mother Śacī,
is unparalleled in rendering expert service to Lord Kṛṣṇa.
> He is that great saintly spiritual master,
most magnanimous within this universe,
> who bestows devotional service to Kṛṣṇa
in various places throughout the world.

(2) *tāra icchā balavān,   pāścātyete ṭhān ṭhān,*
> *haya ya gaurāṅgera nāma*
pṛthivīte nagarādi,   āsamudra nada-nadī,
> *sakhalei laya kṛṣṇa-nāma*

tāra – his; *icchā* – desire; *balavān* – powerful; *pāścātyete* – to the Western world; *ṭhān ṭhān* – everywhere; *haya* – there is; *ya* – in which; *gaurāṅgera nāma* – the name of Gaurāṅga; *pṛthivīte* – on the earth; *nagara-ādi* – towns and so forth; *āsamudra* – extending out to the ocean; *nada-nadī* – rivers and streams; *sakale-i* – verily all; *laya* – taking (chanting); *kṛṣṇa-nāma* – the holy name of Kṛṣṇa.

His desire is very powerful, and thus he is causing
> the holy name of Lord Gaurāṅga to manifest
throughout the countries of the Western world.
> In all the cities, towns, and villages of the earth,
extending to all the oceans, rivers, and streams,
> everyone is chanting the holy name of Kṛṣṇa.

(3) *tāhale ānanda haya,   tabe haya digvijaya,*
> *caitanyera kṛpā atiśaya*
māyā duṣṭa yata duḥkhī,   jagate sabāi sukhī,
> *vaiṣṇavera icchā pūrṇa haya*

tāhale – upon that; *ānanda haya* – there is bliss; *tabe* – then; *haya* – there is; *dik-vijaya* – conquering all directions; *caitanyera kṛpā* – the mercy of Lord Caitanya; *atiśaya* – excessive; *māyā duṣṭa* – corrupted by illusion; *yata* – whichever; *duḥkhī* – miserable souls; *jagate* – in the universe; *sabāi* – everyone; *sukhī* – happy people; *vaiṣṇavera icchā* – the desire of the devotees; *pūrṇa haya* – is fulfilled.

They will become so blissful chanting
    that all directions will be conquered
by Śrī Caitanya Mahāprabhu's abundant mercy.
    When all the miserable living entities in the world
who have been tormented by *māyā* become truly happy,
    then the Vaiṣṇavas' desire will be fulfilled.

(4) *se kārya ye karibāre,   ājñā yadi dile more,*
    yogya nahi ati dīna hīna
tāi se tomāra kṛpā,   jāgiteche anurūpā,
    āji tumi sabāra pravīṇa

se kārya – that task; *ye* – which; *karibāre* – to do; *ājñā* – command; *yadi* – if; *dile* – gave; *more* – to me; *yogya nahi* – not worthy; *ati dīna* – very fallen; *hīna* – destitute; *tāi* – just so; *se* – that; *tomāra* – Your; *kṛpā* – mercy; *jāgiteche* – it is awakening; *anurūpā* – accordingly; *āji* – today; *tumi* – You; *sabāra* – of everyone; *pravīṇa* – wise.

Although my Guru Mahārāja ordered me
    to undertake this mission,
I am unworthy to do it,
    being very fallen and incompetent.
This being the case, O Lord Kṛṣṇa,
    today I am begging for Your mercy
to make me worthy of such a task,
    for Your wisdom is supreme.

(5) *tomāra se śakti pele,   guru-sevā vastu mile,*
    jīvana sārthaka yadi haya
sei se sevā pele,   tāhale sukhī hale,
    tava saṅga bhāgyete milaya

tomāra – Your; *se* – that; *śakti* – potency; *pele* – obtaining; *guru-sevā* – by service to the spiritual master; *vastu* – the real substance (the Absolute Truth); *mile* – gets; *jīvana* – life; *sārthaka* – successful; *yadi haya* – if it is; *sei se* – that particular; *sevā* – service; *pele* – obtaining; *tāhale* – upon that; *sukhī* – happy person; *hale* – becomes; *tava saṅga* – Your association; *bhāgyete* – by good fortune; *milaya* – meets.

If I receive that divine empowerment from You,

    then, by serving my spiritual master, I will attain

the real substance, the Absolute Truth,

    and the purpose of my existence will be fulfilled.

By remaining absorbed in that devotional service,

    I will become truly happy

and by good fortune receive Your personal association.

(6) *evaṁ janaṁ nipatitaṁ prabhavāhi-kūpe*

kāmābhikāmam anu yaḥ prapatan prasaṅgāt

    kṛtvātmasāt surarṣiṇā bhagavan gṛhītaḥ

so 'haṁ kathaṁ nu visṛje tava bhṛtya-sevām

evam – thus; *janam* – people in general; *nipatitam* – fallen; *prabhava* – of material existence; *ahi-kūpe* – in a blind well full of snakes; *kāma-abhikāmam* – lusting after objects of sense gratification; *anu* – following; *yaḥ* – who; *prapatan* – falling down; *prasaṅgāt* – due to bad association; *kṛtvā* – having made; *ātmasāt* – similar to himself; *sura-ṛṣiṇā* – by the great sage Nārada; *bhagavan* – Lord; *gṛhītaḥ* – accepted; *saḥ* – he; *aham* – I; *katham* – how; *nu* – indeed; *visṛje* – can give up; *tava* – Your; *bhṛtya-sevām* – service of Your servant.

[As Prahlāda Mahārāja said to Lord Nṛsiṁhadeva

    in *Śrīmad-Bhāgavatam* (7.9.28):]

"My dear Lord, O Supreme Personality of Godhead!

    By associating with material desires, one after another,

I was following the general populace,

    falling into a blind well full of snakes.

Then the great Nārada Muni kindly accepted me

    as his disciple and instructed me how to achieve

a transcendental position similar to his own.

    How could I ever leave the service of Your servant?"

(7) *tumi mora cira-sāthī,   bhuliyā māyāra lāthi,*

    khāiyāchi janma-janmāntare

āji punaḥ e suyoga,   yadi haya yogāyoga,
tabe pāri tuṅhe milibāre

tumi – You; *mora* – my; *cira-sāthī* – perpetual companion; *bhuliyā* – forgetting; *māyāra* –
of illusion; *lāthi* – kick; *khāiyāchi* – I am suffering; *janma-janmāntare* – birth after birth;
āji – today; *punaḥ* – again; *e* – this; *su-yoga* – opportunity; *yadi haya* – if it is; *yogāyoga*
– association; *tabe* – then; *pāri* – I am able; *tuṅhe milibāre* – to meet You.

O Lord Kṛṣṇa, You are my eternal companion.
    Somehow forgetting about You,
I have been suffering the kicking of *māyā*
    for many, many births.
If today the chance to meet You occurs again,
    then surely I will be able to rejoin You.

(8) *tomāra milane bhāi,   ābāra se sukha pāi,*
        gocāraṇe ghuri dina bhora
    kata vane chuṭāchuṭi,   vane khāi luṭāpuṭi,
        sei dina kabe habe mora

tomāra – Your; *milane* – in the meeting; *bhāi* – O brother; *ābāra* – once more; *se sukha*
– that happiness; *pāi* – I experience; *gocāraṇe* – tending the cows; *ghuri* – I wander; *dina*
bhora – all through the day; *kata vane* – in so many forests; *chuṭāchuṭi* – running and
frolicking; *vane* – in the forest; *khāi*   eating; *luṭāpuṭi*   rolling on the ground; *sei dina* –
that day; *kabe* – when; *habe mora* – it will be mine.

O my dear brother! In Your company
    I will experience great joy once again.
Wandering about the pastures and fields,
    I will pass the entire day with You in tending the cows.
Running and frolicking with You throughout the many forests of Vraja,
    I will roll on the ground in spiritual ecstasy.
    When, oh when, will that day be mine

(9) *āji se subidhāne,   tomāra smaraṇa bhela,*
        baḍa āśā ḍākilāma tāi

ami tomāra nitya-dāsa,   tāi kari eta āsa,
tumi vinā anya gati nāi

āji – today; *se* – that; *su-vidhāne*– in a nice way; *tomāra* – Your; *smaraṇa* – remembrance; *bhela* – happened; *baḍa āśā* – great longing; *ḍākilāma* – I called out; *tāi* – just so; *ami* – I; *tomāra* – Your; *nitya-dāsa* – eternal servant; *tāi* – just so; *kari* – I maintain; *eta āśa* – such a desire; *tumi vinā* – other than You; *anya gati* – another refuge; *nāi* – there is not;

Today that remembrance of being with You
   came to me in a very nice way.
Feeling great longing, I loudly called out to You.
O Lord Kṛṣṇa! Only because I am Your eternal servant
   do I desire Your association so much.
Except for You, I have no other refuge.

Mārkine Bhāgavata Dharma

Mārkine Bhāgavata-Dharma

"Preaching Kṛṣṇa Consciousness in America"
composed by His Divine Grace
A. C. Bhaktivedanta Swami Prabhupāda
aboard the *Jaladuta*, on September 18, 1965

INTRODUCTION

After a thirty-five-day journey from Calcutta, the *Jaladuta* reached Boston's Commonwealth Pier at 5:30 A.M. on September 17, 1965. The ship was to stop briefly in Boston before proceeding to New York City. Among the first things Śrīla Prabhupāda saw in America when the sun came up were the letters "A & P" painted on a pierfront warehouse. The gray waterfront dawn revealed the ships in the harbor, a conglomeration of lobster stands and drab buildings, and, rising in the distance, the Boston skyline.

Prabhupāda had to pass through U.S. Customs and Immigration in Boston. His visa allowed him a three-month stay. Captain Pandia invited Prabhupāda to take a walk into Boston, where the captain intended to do some shopping. They walked across a footbridge into a busy commercial area with old churches, warehouses, office buildings, bars, tawdry bookshops, nightclubs, and restaurants. Prabhupāda briefly observed the city, but the most significant thing about his short stay in Boston, aside from the fact that he had now set foot in America, was that at Commonwealth Pier he wrote another poem in Bengali, entitled *Mārkine Bhāgavata-Dharma:* "Preaching Kṛṣṇa Consciousness in America".

He was now in America, in a major city, rich with billions, populated with millions, and not likely to welcome "new" spiritual ideas. Prabhupāda saw Boston from the viewpoint of a pure devotee of Kṛṣṇa. He saw the hellish city life, people dedicated to the illusion of material happiness. All his dedication and training moved him to give these people the transcendental knowledge and saving grace of Kṛṣṇa consciousness, yet he was feeling weak, ill-suited, and incapable of helping them on his own. He was but "an insignificant beggar" with no money. He had barely survived the two heart attacks at sea, he spoke a different language, he dressed strangely – yet he had come to tell people to give up their meat-eating, illicit sex, intoxication, and gambling, and to teach them how to worship Lord Kṛṣṇa, who to them was only a mythical Hindu god. What would he be able to accomplish?

In helplessness, he spoke his heart directly to God: "*O Lord, please bestow Your mercy so that under Your divine guidance/ I may be able to persuade them of Your message.*" And for convincing them he would trust in the power of God's holy name and in *Śrīmad-Bhāgavatam*. These transcendental sounds would clean away desire for material enjoyment from their hearts and awaken desire for loving service to Kṛṣṇa. On the streets of Boston, Prabhupāda was aware of the powers of ignorance and passion that dominated the city, but he had firm faith in the transcendental process. He was tiny; God was infinite – and God was Kṛṣṇa, his dearmost friend.

Śrīla Prabhupāda was dressed appropriately for a resident of Vṛndāvana. He wore *kaṇṭhi-mālā* (neck beads) and a simple cotton *dhotī*, and he carried *japa-mālā* (chanting beads) and an old *chādar*, or shawl. His complexion was golden, his head shaven, *śikhā* tuft in the back, his forehead decorated with the whitish Vaiṣṇava *tilaka*. He wore pointed white rubber slippers, not uncommon for *sādhus* in India. But even though city dwellers have a natural tendency to ignore any kind of strange new arrival, who in Boston had ever seen or dreamed of anyone appearing like this Vaiṣṇava? He was possibly the first Vaiṣṇava *sannyāsī* to arrive in America with a totally uncompromised appearance.

After the steamship left Boston and arrived in New York City, Śrīla Prabhupāda was on his own. He had a sponsor, Gopal Agarwal, somewhere in Pennsylvania. Surely someone would be here to greet him. Although he had little idea of what to do as he walked off the ship onto the pier – "I did not know whether to turn left or right" – he passed through the dockside formalities and was met by a representative from Traveler's Aid, sent by Mr. Agarwal, who offered to take him to the Scindia ticket office in Manhattan to book his return passage to India.

At the Scindia office, Prabhupāda spoke with the ticket agent, Joseph Foerster, who was impressed by this unusual passenger's Vaiṣṇava appearance, his light luggage, and his apparent poverty. He regarded Prabhupāda as a priest. Most of Scindia's passengers were businessmen or families, so Mr. Foerster had never seen a passenger wearing the traditional Vaiṣṇava dress of India. He found Śrīla Prabhupāda to be "a pleasant gentleman" who spoke of "the nice accommodations and treatment he had received aboard the *Jaladuta*." Prabhupāda asked Mr. Foerster to hold space for him on a return ship to India. His plans were to leave in about two months, and he told Mr. Foerster that he would keep in touch. Carrying only forty rupees cash, which he himself called "a few hours' spending in New York," and an additional twenty dollars he had collected from selling three volumes of the *Bhāgavatam* to Captain Pandia, Śrīla Prabhupāda, with umbrella and suitcase in hand, and still escorted by the Traveler's Aid representative, set out for the Port Authority Bus Terminal to arrange for his trip to Butler, Pennsylvania.

Mārkine Bhāgavata-Dharma

"Preaching Kṛṣṇa Consciousness in America"

(1)   *baḍa-kṛpā kaile kṛṣṇa! adhamera prati*
       ki lāgiyā nile hethā kara ebe gati

baḍa-kṛpā – great mercy; *kaile* – showed; *kṛṣṇa* – O Lord Kṛṣṇa; *adhamera prati* – to this fallen soul; *ki lāgiyā* – for what reason; *nile* – You have brought me; *hethā* – here; *kara* – please show; *ebe* – now; *gati* – Your purpose.

> My dear Lord Kṛṣṇa, You have shown
>   great kindness to this useless soul.
> Why have You brought me here?
>   Now You can fulfill Your own purpose
> by doing whatever You like with me.

(2)   *āche kichu kārya tava ei anumāne*
       nahe kena ānibena ei ugra-sthāne

āche – there is; *kichu* – some; *kārya* – work; *tava* – Your; *ei* – this; *anumāne* – by guessing; *nahe* – if not; *kena* – why; *ānibena* – You have brought; *ei ugra-sthāne* – to this horrible place.

> I can guess that You have some work to do here;
>   otherwise, why would You bring me
> to this terrible place?

(3)   *rajos tamo guṇe erā sabāi ācchanna*
       vāsudeva-kathā ruci nahe se prasanna

rajaḥ – the mode of passion; *tamaḥ* – the mode of ignorance; *guṇe* – by the modes; *erā* – their; *sabāi* – all of them; *ācchanna* – covered; *vāsudeva-kathā* – topics about Lord Kṛṣṇa, the son of Vasudeva; *ruci* – taste; *nahe* – not; *se* – they; *prasanna* – are pleased.

> Most of the people here are covered
>   by the material modes of passion and ignorance.

They take no pleasure in hearing transcendental topics
about Lord Kṛṣṇa, the son of Vasudeva.

(4)   *tabe yadi tava kṛpā haya ahaitukī*
      sakali sambhava haya tumi se kautukī

tabe – then; *yadi* – if; *tava* – Your; *kṛpā* – mercy; *haya* – is shown; *ahaitukī* – causeless;
sakali – all things; *sambhava haya* – it is possible; *tumi* – You; *se* – such; *kautukī* – fond
of amusements.

But I know that all things are possible
      when You show Your causeless mercy,
because You are so playful
      and fond of inconceivable pastimes.

(5)   *ki bhāve bujhāle tārā bujhe sei rasa*
      eta kṛpā kara prabhu kari nija-vaśa

ki bhāve – in what manner; *bujhāle* – causing to understand; *tārā* – them; *bujhe* –
comprehending; *sei rasa* – that mellow; *eta* – such as this; *kṛpā* – mercy; *kara* – please
display; *prabhu* – O Lord; *kari* – making; *nija-vaśa* – under Your controlling power.

How can I help them to comprehend
      the transcendental mellows of devotional service?
O Lord, please bestow Your mercy so that under Your divine guidance
      I may be able to persuade them of Your message.

(6)   *tomāra icchāya saba haya māyā-vaśa*
      tomāra icchāya nāśa māyāra paraśa

tomāra icchāya – according to Your desire; *saba* – everyone; *haya* – is; *māyā-vaśa* –
controlled by illusion; *tomāra icchāya* – according to Your desire; *nāśa* – destruction;
māyāra paraśa – the touch of illusion.

By Your will, all living entities in this world have fallen
      under the control of the illusory energy.
By Your will, they can also be set free
      from that illusion's clutches.

(7)   *tava icchā haya yadi tādera uddhāra*
   bujhibe niścai tabe kathā se tomāra

tava icchā – Your desire; *haya* – is; *yadi* – if; *tādera* – their; *uddhāra* – deliverance; *bujhibe* – they will comprehend; *niścai* – definitely; *tabe* – then; *kathā* – message; *se* – that; *tomāra* – Your.

Therefore if it is Your wish
   for them to be delivered,
then surely they will be able
   to comprehend Your message.

(8)   *bhāgavatera kathā se' tava avatāra*
   dhīra hañā śune yadi kāne bāra bāra

bhāgavatera kathā – the message of *Śrīmad-Bhāgavatam*; *se'* – that; *tava avatāra* – Your incarnation; *dhīra hañā* – becoming grave; *śune* – by hearing; *yadi* – if; *kāne* – in the ear; *bāra bāra* – again and again.

The transcendental narrations found in the *Śrīmad-Bhāgavatam*
   are Your direct literary incarnation.
If a person becomes serious about spiritual life
   and repeatedly listens to these narrations
with submissive aural reception, then he will understand.

(9)   *śṛṇvatāṁ sva-kathāḥ kṛṣṇaḥ*
       puṇya-śravaṇa-kīrtanaḥ
       hṛdy antaḥ-stho hy adhadrāṇi
       vidhunoti suhṛt satām

śṛṇvatām – those who want to hear the message; *sva-kathāḥ* – His own words; *kṛṣṇaḥ* – the Personality of Godhead; *puṇya* – virtuous; *śravaṇa-kīrtanaḥ* – hearing and chanting; *hṛdi* – in the heart; *antaḥ-sthaḥ* – situated within; *hi* – certainly; *adhadrāṇi* – inauspicious things [desires to enjoy matter]; *vidhunoti* – cleanses; *suhṛt* – the benefactor; *satām* – of the truthful devotee.

[As stated in *Śrīmad-Bhāgavatam* (1.2.17–21):]

"Śrī Kṛṣṇa, the Personality of Godhead,
>   who is the benefactor of the truthful devotee,
cleanses inauspicious desires for material enjoyment
>   from the heart of the devotee who relishes His messages,
which are in themselves virtuous
>   when properly heard and chanted."

> *naṣṭa-prāyeṣv abhadreṣu*
> > *nityaṁ bhāgavata-sevayā*
> *bhagavaty uttama-śloke*
> > *bhaktir bhavati naiṣṭhikī*

naṣṭa – destroyed; *prāyeṣu* – almost completely; *abhadreṣu* – all inauspicious things; *nityam* – regularly; *bhāgavata-sevayā* – by serving the book *Bhāgavata* or person *Bhāgavata*; *bhagavati* – unto the Personality of Godhead; *uttama-śloke* – unto He who is glorified with exalted verses; *bhaktiḥ* – loving devotional service; *bhavati* – comes into being; *naiṣṭhikī* – irrevocable.

"By regularly hearing recitations of the book *Bhāgavatam*
>   and rendering service unto the pure devotee (**bhāgavata**),
all inauspicious things that are troublesome
>   to the heart are practically destroyed.
Then loving devotional service unto the glorious Lord,
>   who is praised with transcendental songs,
is established as an irrevocable fact."

> *tadā rajas-tamo bhāvāḥ*
> > *kāma-lobhādayaś ca ye*
> *ceta etair anāviddhaṁ*
> > *sthitaṁ sattve prasīdati*

tadā – at that time; *rajaḥ-tamaḥ* – the modes of passion and ignorance; *bhāvāḥ* – the situation; *kāma-lobha-ādayaḥ* – lust, greed, and so forth; *ca* – also; *ye* – whatever; *cetaḥ* – the consciousness; *etaiḥ* – by these; *anāviddham* – without being affected; *sthitam* – being fixed; *sattve* – in the mode of goodness; *prasīdati* – becomes satisfied.

"At the time loving service is established in the heart,
the modes of passion and ignorance,
as well as the urges of lust, greed, and so forth
disappear from the heart.
Then the devotee is situated in goodness,
and he becomes completely happy."

evaṁ prasanna-manaso
bhagavad-bhakti-yogataḥ
bhagavat-tattva-vijñānaṁ
mukta-saṅgasya jāyate

evam – thus; *prasanna-manasaḥ* – whose consciousness is pleased; *bhagavat-bhakti-yogataḥ* – by contact with devotional service to the Lord; *bhagavat-tattva-vijñānam* – realization of the truth regarding the Personality of Godhead; *mukta* – liberated; *saṅgasya* – of the association; *jāyate* – becomes effective.

"Thus happily established in the mode of unalloyed goodness,
the devotee whose heart has been enlivened
by contact with loving devotional service to the Lord
gains scientific realization of the truth
regarding the Personality of Godhead.
This is effected in the stage of
liberation from all material association."

bhidyate hṛdaya-granthiś
chidyante sarva-saṁśayāḥ
kṣīyante cāsya karmāṇi
dṛṣṭa evātmanīśvare

bhidyate – pierced; *hṛdaya-granthiḥ* – the knot in the heart; *chidyante* – cut to pieces; *sarva-saṁśayāḥ* – all doubts; *kṣīyante* – terminated; *ca* – and; *asya* – his; *karmāṇi* – fruitive reactions; *dṛṣṭa* – having seen; *eva* – certainly; *ātmani* – unto the self; *īśvare* – dominating.

"The knot in the heart is pierced,
    and all spiritual doubts are cut to pieces.
The sequence of fruitive actions and reactions
    is terminated when one finally sees
the spirit self as the true master."

(10)   *rajas tamo ha'te tabe pāibe nistāra*
          hṛdayera abhadra saba ghucibe tāhāra

rajaḥ – the mode of passion; *tamaḥ* – the mode of ignorance; *ha'te* – from; *tabe* – then; *pāibe* – will attain; *nistāra* – deliverance; *hṛdayera* – of the heart; *abhadra* – inauspicious; *saba* – all; *ghucibe* – will be removed; *tāhāra* – their.

By this process the people will be liberated from the influence
    of the modes of passion and ignorance,
and all inauspicious things accumulated
    in the core of the heart will be dissolved.

(11)   *ki kare bujhāba kathā vara sei cāhi*
          kṣudra āmi dīna hīna kona śakti nāhi

ki kare – by doing what; *bujhāba* – I will make them understand; *kathā* – Your message; *vara* – benediction; *sei* – that; *cāhi* – I crave; *kṣudra* – tiny; *āmi* – I; *dīna hīna* – fallen and insignificant; *kona śakti* – any power; *nāhi* – there is not.

O Lord! What should I do to help them understand
    this transcendental message of the *Bhāgavatam?*
I need Your merciful benediction to persuade them,
    for I am very unfortunate, unqualified, and the most fallen;
I have no power to do so on my own.

(12)   *athaca enecho prabhu! kathā balibāre*
          ye tomāra icchā haya kara ei-bāre

athaca – nevertheless; *enecho* – You have brought; *prabhu* – O Lord; *kathā* – message; *balibāre* – to speak; *ye* – which; *tomāra icchā* – Your will; *haya* – it is; *kara* – please do; *ei-bāre* – now.

In spite of my shortcomings, O Lord,
>   You have somehow brought me to this country
just to speak about You.
>   Now it is up to You, O Lord,
to make me a success or failure, as You like.

(13)   *akhila jagata-guru! vacana se āmāra*
>   *alaṅkṛta karibāra kṣamatā tomāra*

akhila jagata-guru – O spiritual master of the entire universe; *vacana* – words; *se* – that; *āmāra* – my; *alaṅkṛta* – decorated; *karibāra* – to make; *kṣamatā* – the ability; *tomāra* – Your.

O spiritual master of all the worlds!
>   Only You have the power to enhance my words
and thereby make them suitable
>   for everyone's understanding.

(14)   *tava kṛpā ha'le mora kathā śuddha habe*
>   *śuniyā sabāra śoka-duḥkha ye ghucibe*

tava kṛpā – Your mercy; *ha'le* – upon showing; *mora kathā* – my speech; *śuddha habe* – will become pure; *śuniyā* – hearing; *sabāra* – of everyone; *śoka-duḥkha* – lamentation and misery; *ye* – which; *ghucibe* – will be removed.

Only when You bestow Your causeless mercy upon me
>   will my words become transcendentally pure.
By hearing these messages, all the people
>   will certainly feel enlivened and thus be relieved
of their miserable condition of life.

(15)   *āniyācha yadi tumi āmāre nācāte*
>   *nācāo nācāo prabhu nācāo se-mate*

āniyācha – have brought; *yadi* – if; *tumi* – You; *āmāre* – to me; *nācāte* – cause to dance; *nācāo* – make me dance; *nācāo* – make me dance; *prabhu* – O Lord; *nācāo* – make me dance; *se-mate* – in that manner.

If You have brought me here to dance, O Lord,
then make me dance, make me dance.
O Lord, make me dance as You like.

(16) *bhakti nāi veda nāi nāme khuba baḍa*
"bhaktivedānta" nāma ebe sārthak kara

bhakti nāi – there is no devotion; *veda nāi* – there is no knowledge; *nāme* – by the title; *khuba baḍa* – very big [inappropriately exalted]; *bhaktivedānta nāma* – the name Bhaktivedanta; *ebe* – now; *sārthak kara* – please fulfill it.

Although I have no devotion (**bhakti**), nor any knowledge (**vedānta**),
still I have been inappropriately honored
with the lofty title "Bhaktivedānta."
Now if You like, O Lord, You can fulfill
the real purport of that name.

—The most unfortunate, insignificant beggar, Bhaktivedanta Swami, onboard the ship *Jaladuta*, Commonwealth Pier, Boston, Massachusetts (U.S.A.). Dated 18th of September, 1965.

Śrī Keśava
Praṇāma Śloka

Śrī Keśava Praṇāma Śloka

"Eulogy in Sanskrit Verse"
composed on October 21, 1968, by
His Divine Grace A. C. Bhaktivedanta Swami Prabhupāda
in honor of the disappearance of
his godbrother and *sannyāsa guru,*
Śrī Śrīmad Bhakti-prajñāna Keśava Gosvāmī Mahārāja

vairāgya-vidyā-nija-bhakti-yogam
apāyayan mām anabhīpsum andham
śri-keśava-bhakti-prajñāna-nāma
kṛpāmbudhir yas tam ahaṁ prapadye

vairāgya-vidyā – the knowledge of transcendental renunciation; *nija* – his own [Lord Caitanya's]; *bhakti-yogam* – devotional service; *apāyayan* – has caused to drink; *mām* – me; *anabhīpsum* – unwilling; *andham* – a blind person; *śrī-keśava-bhakti-prajñāna-nāmaḥ* – named Śrī Bhakti-prajñāna Keśava Gosvāmī; *kṛpā-ambudhiḥ* – an ocean of mercy; *yaḥ* – who; *tam* – to him; *aham prapadye* – I offer my respectful obeisances.

I was completely blind, unwilling to drink the medicine
of Kṛṣṇa consciousness, which is endowed with knowledge
of transcendental detachment from this material world.
But my godbrother Śrī Bhakti-prajñāna Keśava Mahārāja
forcefully made me drink this medicine.
He showed this favor upon me because he is an ocean of mercy.
I offer my respectful obeisances unto Him.

OFFERING CONDOLENCES

By September of 1968, Śrīla Prabhupāda had made much progress in his preaching mission. From the initial period of struggling alone in the New York winter of 1965–66, he had established several temples in America and beyond. His movement was quickly becoming a worldwide happening. On September 21, 1968, Prabhupāda flew from San Francisco to Seattle, Washington, to oversee the foundation of a new Hare Kṛṣṇa temple. He stayed there until his departure for Montreal a month later.

On October 21, two days before his departure from Seattle, Śrīla Prabhupāda received a telegram from Śrīla Bhaktivedānta Trivikrama Mahārāja, a prominent disciple of Śrī Śrīmad Bhakti-prajñāna Keśava Gosvāmī Mahārāja, informing him of Keśava Mahārāja's disappearance from this world on October 6. Stricken with this grievous news, Śrīla Prabhupāda immediately wrote a letter of condolence for Keśava Mahārāja's disciples. Within it he composed a Sanskrit *śloka* that expresses in poetic Vaiṣṇava imagery his gratitude to his dear godbrother Keśava Mahārāja for forcing him to leave householder life and become a *sannyāsī*.

There are several interesting features of the Sanskrit *praṇāma śloka* that Śrīla Prabhupāda composed for Keśava Mahārāja. Parts of it were directly inspired by two verses in the Vaiṣṇava scriptures. The first and fourth lines are the same as those of a famous *śloka* composed by Sārvabhauma Bhaṭṭācārya in glorification of Śrī Caitanya Mahāprabhu, as found in the *Caitanya-candrodaya-nāṭaka*, by Śrī Kavi-karṇapura:

> *vairāgya-vidyā-nija-bhakti-yoga-*
> *śikṣārtham ekaḥ puruṣaḥ purāṇaḥ*
> *śrī-kṛṣṇa-caitanya-śarīra-dhārī*
> *kṛpāmbudhir yas tam ahaṁ prapadye*

"Let me take shelter of the Supreme Personality of Godhead, Śrī Kṛṣṇa, who has descended in the form of Lord Caitanya Mahāprabhu to teach us real knowledge, His devotional service, and detachment from whatever does not foster Kṛṣṇa consciousness. He has descended because He is an ocean of transcendental mercy. Let me surrender unto His lotus feet."

This verse is quoted in the *Śrī Caitanya-caritāmṛta*, Madhya-līlā 6.254 and was also quoted by Śrīla Prabhupāda many times in his lectures and conversations.

The second line of Śrīla Prabhupāda's verse – *apāyayan mām anabhīpsum andham* – is the same as the second line of a verse found in Śrīla Raghunātha Dāsa Gosvāmī's famous prayer *Vilāpa-kusumāñjali*, verse six, wherein he expresses his obligation to Śrīla Sanātana Gosvāmī in the following words:

> *vairāgya-yug-bhakti-rasaṁ prayatnair*
> *apāyayan mām anabhīpsum andham*
> *kṛpāmbudhir yaḥ para-duḥkha-duḥkhī*
> *sanātanaṁ taṁ prabhum āśrayāmi*

"I was blind, unwilling to drink the nectar of devotional service endowed with renunciation. But Sanātana Gosvāmī, out of his causeless mercy, made me drink it, even though I was otherwise unable to do so. Therefore he is an ocean of mercy. He is very compassionate to fallen souls like me, and thus it is my duty to offer my respectful obeisances unto his lotus feet."

This verse is quoted by Śrīla Prabhupāda in his purport to *Śrī Caitanya-caritāmṛta*, *Ādi-līlā* 5.203.

Srila Prabhupāda had given a lecture at the temple as usual that evening in Seattle, and then returned to his apartment, where he had received the news of Keśava Mahārāja's disappearance. The devotees at the temple had taken hot milk and were preparing themselves for rest, when suddenly Prabhupāda reentered the temple. It was unusual. The devotees offered obeisances and waited in keen anticipation. Prabhupāda's mood was very grave. He again sat on the *vyāsāsana* and asked them to sit. He had his servant adjust the tape recorder and play a tape of his own singing and playing the harmonium. Puzzled, the devotees looked at one another. For about thirty minutes, a beautiful *bhajana* of Prabhupāda singing the "*Vande 'haṁ*" prayers played in the room before the assembled devotees.

When it ended, Prabhupāda said, "I have just received one telegram from India. The person who gave me *sannyāsa* has left his body. One has to accept the renounced order from another person who is in the renounced order. So I never thought that I shall accept this renounced order of life. In my family life, when I was in the midst of my wife and children, sometimes I was dreaming my spiritual master, that he's calling me, and I was following him. When my dream was over, I was thinking, I was little horrified, 'Oh, Guru Mahārāja wants me to become a *sannyāsī*. How can I accept *sannyāsa*?' At that time, I was feeling not very satisfied that I have to give up my family and become a mendicant. At that time, it was a horrible feeling. Sometimes I was thinking, 'No, I cannot take *sannyāsa*.' But again I saw the same dream. So in this way I was fortunate. My Guru Mahārāja [*Prabhupāda's voice chokes*] he pulled me out from this material life. [*For several moments Prabhupāda could not speak, and everyone present saw tears come from his eyes.*]

"I have not lost anything. He was so kind upon me. I have gained. I left three children; I have got now three hundred children. So I am not loser. This is material conception. We think that we shall be loser by accepting Kṛṣṇa. Nobody is loser. I say from my practical experience. I was thinking that 'How can I accept this renounced order of life? I cannot accept so much trouble.' So . . . but I retired from my family life.

"I was sitting alone in Vṛndāvana, writing books. So this, my godbrother, he insisted to me, 'Bhaktivedanta Prabhu . . .' This title was given in my family life. It was offered to me by the Vaiṣṇava society. So he insisted. Not *he* insisted – practically my spiritual master insisted *through* him, that 'You accept.' Because without accepting the renounced order of life, nobody can become a preacher. So he wanted me to become a preacher. So he forced me through this godbrother: 'You accept.' So unwillingly I accepted. And then I remembered that he wanted me to go to the Western country. So I am feeling now very much obliged to this godbrother, that he carried out the wish of my spiritual master and forced me to accept this *sannyāsa* order.

So this godbrother, His Holiness Keśava Mahārāja, is no more. He has entered Kṛṣṇa's abode. So I wish to pass a resolution of bereavement and send it. And I have composed one verse also in this connection in Sanskrit. So you all present, you sign this. I shall send it tomorrow.

The verse I have composed, it is in Sanskrit: *vairāgya-vidyā-nija-bhakti-yogam*. This Kṛṣṇa consciousness is *vairāgya-vidyā*. *Vairāgya-vidyā* means to become detestful to this material world. That is called *vairāgya-vidyā*. And that is possible simply by this *bhakti-yoga. Vairāgya-vidyā-nija-bhakti-yogam apāyayan mām.*

So just like medicine, the child is afraid of taking medicine. That also I have experienced. In my childhood, when I became ill, I was very stubborn; I wouldn't accept any medicine. So my mother used to force medicine within my mouth with a spoon. I was so obstinate. So anyway, similarly, I did not want to accept this *sannyāsa* order, but this godbrother forced me. 'You must.' *Apāyayan mām:* he forcefully made me to drink this medicine. *Anabhīpsum andham.* Why I was unwilling? *Anabhīpsu* means 'unwilling'. *Andham, andham* means 'one who is blind, who cannot see his future'. The spiritual life is the brightest future, but the materialists cannot see it. You see? But the Vaiṣṇavas, the spiritual masters, they forcefully: 'You drink this medicine.' You see? *Apāyayan mām anabhīpsum andham śrī-keśava-bhakti-prajñāna-nāma.*

So my godbrother, his name is Keśava, Bhakti-prajñāna Keśava. *Kṛpāmbudhi.* So he did this favor upon me because he was an ocean of mercy. So we offer our obeisances to the Vaiṣṇava, *kṛpāmbudhi.*

vāñchā-kalpa-tarubhyaś ca kṛpā-sindhubhya eva ca.

The Vaiṣṇavas, the representatives of the Lord, are so kind. They bring the ocean of mercy for distributing to the suffering humanity. *Kṛpāmbudhir yas tam aham prapadye.* So I am offering my respectful obeisances unto His Holiness, because he forcefully made me adopt this *sannyāsa* order.

So he is no more in this world. He has entered Kṛṣṇa's abode. So I am offering my respectful obeisances along with my disciples. On the first day of my *sannyāsa,* I never thought, but I remembered that I'll have to speak in English. So I remember on that *sannyāsa* day, when there was a reception, so I, first of all, I spoke in English. So it is all arrangement of Kṛṣṇa, higher authority. We are writing like this:

"Resolved, that we the undersigned members and devotees of International Society for Krishna Consciousness Incorporated, in a condolence meeting under the presidency of His Divine Grace A. C. Bhaktivedanta Swami, today the 21st of October, 1968, at our Seattle branch, express our profound bereavement on hearing of the passing of His

Divine Grace Oṁ Viṣṇupāda Śrī Śrīmad Bhakti-prajñāna Keśava Gosvāmī Mahārāja (the *sannyāsa guru*, preceptor of our spiritual master), as of October 6th, 1968, at his headquarter residence in Nabadwip, West Bengal, India. We offer our respectful obeisances unto the lotus feet of Śrī Śrīmad B. P. Keśava Gosvāmī Mahārāja with the following verse composed on this occasion by our spiritual master."

This verse I have already explained to you. So I wish that you all sign this, and I'll send it tomorrow by airmail. Have you got a pencil?

Govinda Dāsī: Yes [*sound of Prabhupāda signing*].

Prabhupāda first signed his own name and then gave the letter to Kārtikeya to take to each devotee in the room. One by one, they placed the paper on the floor and signed it. The devotee carrying the paper was about to pass by several guests, but Prabhupāda said, "No, no. Everyone here is present, and so they are all a witness." The last one to sign was Prabhupāda's servant, Kārtikeya. He put the paper on the floor and slowly signed his name, while Śrīla Prabhupāda leaned forward on the *vyāsāsana*, watching very intently.

Among those present on this occasion were Govinda Dāsī, Jayānanda Dāsa Brahmacārī, Madhudviṣa Dāsa Brahmacārī, Viṣṇujana Dāsa Brahmacārī, Tamāla-kṛṣṇa Dāsa Brahmacārī, Jāhnavā Dāsī, Mādhavī-latā Dāsī, Śrīmatī Dāsī, Harṣarāṇī Dāsī, Amala-kṛṣṇa Dāsa Brahmacārī, Revatīnandana Dāsa Brahmacārī, Jīvānanda Dāsa, Sudāmā Dāsa Brahmacārī, Nara-nārāyaṇa Dāsa Brahmacārī, Upendra Dāsa Brahmacārī, Jaya Gopāla Dāsa Brahmacārī, and Kārtikeya Dāsa Brahmacārī.

The next day, October 22, 1968, Śrīla Prabhupāda replied to Śrīla Bhaktivedānta Trivikrama Mahārāja by writing him a nice condolence letter in Bengali. Prabhupāda asked for details about the disappearance of Śrī Śrīmad Bhakti-prajñāna Keśava Gosvāmī Mahārāja, and he fondly described the other dear devotees in India who were close to Keśava Mahārāja. Then he reminded Trivikrama Mahārāja that he (Śrīla Prabhupāda) was one of the three founding members of Keśava Mahārāja's preaching movement, the Śrī Gauḍīya Vedānta Samiti, and was even made president of its Bengali magazine, *Śrī Gauḍīya Patrikā*, and Hindi magazine, *Śrī Bhāgavata Patrikā*. He described how Keśava Mahārāja so compassionately made him a *sannyāsī*, even though he had taken a vow to never accept *sannyāsa*. Then Prabhupāda briefly described his worldwide preaching activities on behalf of Śrī Caitanya Mahāprabhu. And he recalled his last visit with the bedridden Keśava Mahārāja in Calcutta. Prabhupāda even asked Trivikrama Mahārāja to help arrange five acres of land in Śrīdhāma Māyāpura for an *āśrama*, so that "American boys and girls can visit and stay there and receive proper training."

Finally, in the postscript, Śrīla Prabhupāda asked for a nice photograph of Śrīla Keśava Mahārāja in order to have life-size paintings made for placing "in my prominent centers, particularly New York, Hollywood, London and so forth."

This Bengali letter was later translated into Hindi by Śrīla Keśava Mahārāja's disciples and published in the December 1968 issue of *Śrī Bhāgavata Patrikā* along with Śrīla Prabhupāda's letter of condolence, containing the Sanskrit *praṇāma śloka* and the legal and initiated names of his American disciples.

Gratitude to Devotees

We wish to thank some of the many devotees who helped in the endeavors over twelve years to bring out this book:

✳ Prabhus Ranjit, Ekanātha, and other devotees at the Bhaktivedanta Archives.

✳ Śrī Bhakti-Vikāsa Swami for a new computer and for vigilant and helpful editorial suggestions.

✳ The assembly of Bengali devotees, including Śaśimukhī, Akhilāt-mānanda, Anup, Acyutānanda, Makhanchor, Sudarśana, Rādhikā Ramana, and the rest, who patiently answered many questions on the idioms and the figures of speech Śrīla Prabhupāda used in his poetry.

✳ C. V. for empowered editing assistance, which revealed Śrīla Prabhupāda's personal presence and rewarding intervention.

✳ Prabhu Nanda Kishore for the book's title, *A Shower of Divine Compassion*, adapted from the fourth verse of Śrīla Prabhupāda's Invocation from the *Gītāra Gāna*.

✳ Mātājī Jāhnavā for sharing her deep conviction about the much-needed truths of Śrīla Prabhupāda's poems and her artistic suggestions.

✳ Anuradha Devī Dāsī for her exquisite pencil, charcoal, and pastel portraits of Śrīla Prabhupāda.

✳ Prabhu Kūrma Rūpa for the design and layout.

✳ Satsvarūpa Dāsa Goswami for his deep observations and appreciation in the Foreword.

✳ Prabhu Kalakantha, whose vision, faith, and causeless mercy got this project going.

✳ Bhakti Vaikhanas Swami for diligently locating rare or lost manuscripts of Śrīla Prabhupāda's poetry in India.

✳ Bhakti Caru Swami for translating the refrain of "Prayer to the Lotus Feet of Kṛṣṇa".

✳ Prabhu Bhīma, at the Mumbai BBT, for his saintly patience and inspiring perseverance to complete project.

✳ Prabhu Tattvavit for editing the book for the BBT.